Nicole Elert, Christopher T. Brooks
German Employment Law

Nicole Elert,
Christopher T. Brooks

German Employment Law

618 Questions Frequently Asked by Foreigners

DE GRUYTER

Dr. iur. **Nicole Elert**, Lawyer (Rechtsanwältin) and Specialist Lawyer (Fachanwältin) for Employment Law, Partner, PricewaterhouseCoopers Aktiengesellschaft Wirtschaftsprüfungsgesellschaft.

Prof. Dr. phil. **Christopher T. Brooks**, East Stroudsburg University, Pennsylvania.

Recommended form of citation: *Elert/Brooks*, Part 2 Chapter 3 Question 19.

ISBN 978-3-11-030276-9
e-ISBN 978-3-11-030282-0

Bibliographic information published by the Deutsche Nationalbibliothek
The Deutsche Nationalbibliothek lists this publication in the Deutsche Nationalbibliografie; detailed bibliographic data are available in the Internet at http://dnb.d-nb.de.

Data Conversion: jürgen ullrich typosatz, 86720 Nördlingen
Printing and Binding: Hubert & Co. GmbH & Co. KG, Göttingen
♾ Printed on acid-free paper
Printed in Germany

www.degruyter.com

Preface

The number of foreign firms operating in Germany is growing, and so is the number of questions posed by those firms' HR, tax and legal departments, as well as foreign CEOs, investors and even regular employees. Some ask, for example, what is a works council? What is an employer's association? Other issues queried about include – but are certainly not limited to – those regarding freelancers, representation of the disabled, employer associations, how German law is applied to employment relationships between Germans and foreigners, how those employment relationships start and end. With respect to these issues, questions often arise regarding visas and work permits and what legal protections German law affords employers and employees, especially those about equal treatment and dismissal legislation, as well as collective bargaining, parental and maternity issues. In short, German Employment Law is always of great significance, and the core substance of these questions finds its way into corporate boardrooms time and time again.

With this in view, this handbook will serve to answer as simply as possible the questions most commonly posed by those doing business with Germany. The focus of this book is to pose questions that foreigners would commonly ask and then answer them accordingly. We aimed to phrase the questions in a way that an English speaker would formulate them (Note: American English has been chosen for this book). It is a reference book, one that aims to come from a non-German legal perspective. It will work as an introduction to German Employment Law and highlight and explain basic terms that are known to non-Germans (i.e. employer, employee, trade union) as well as those which are not so widely understood (i.e. works council, employers' association). The questions are constructed with a view to the lifecycle of an employment relationship.

When appropriate laws are mentioned, cited or both. However, as the intent of this work is not for it to be a typical law book, many of the specific citations and references have been left out because they will be of little interest to our target audience.

Questions and amendments are kindly asked to be addressed to:
Nicole Elert – nicole.elert@de.pwc.com
Christopher T. Brooks – chrisbrooks@thebillholland.com

Düsseldorf/East Stroudsburg, November 2013

Nicole Elert, Christopher T. Brooks

Content

List of Abbreviations

%	percent
€	Euro
§	section
Abs.	Absatz
AEntG	Arbeitnehmer-Entsendegesetz
AG	Aktiengesellschaft
AGB	Allgemeine Geschäftsbedingungen
AGG	Allgemeines Gleichbehandlungsgesetz
aka	also known as
AÜG	Arbeitnehmerüberlassungsgesetz
BAG	Bundesarbeitsgericht
BBiG	Berufsbildungsgesetz
BDSG	Bundesdatenschutzgesetz
BEEG	Bundeselterngeld- und Elternzeitgesetz
BetrVG	Betriebsverfassungsgesetz
BGB	Bürgerliches Gesetzbuch
BMAS	Bundesministerium für Arbeit und Soziales
BUrlG	Bundesurlaubsgesetz
CEO	Chief Executive Officer
coll.	colloquial
CV	curriculum vitae
dbb	Deutscher Beamtenbund
DGB	Deutscher Gewerkschaftsbund
e.g.	for example
EEA	European Economic Area
etc.	et cetera
EU	European Union
GewO	Gewerbeordnung
GM	General Manager
GmbH	Gesellschaft mit beschränkter Haftung
HGB	Handelsgesetzbuch
HR	human resources
i.e.	that is
IT	information technology
KGaA	Kommanditgesellschaft auf Aktien
KSchG	Kündigungsschutzgesetz
MuSchArbV	Mutterschutzarbeitsplatzverordnung

NachwG	Nachweisgesetz
no.	number
OECD	Organisation for Economic Co-operation and Development
para.	paragraph
SCHUFA	Schutzgemeinschaft für allgemeine Kreditsicherung
sec.	section
SGB III	Sozialgesetzbuch III – Arbeitsförderung
SGB IV	Sozialgesetzbuch IV – Gemeinsame Vorschriften für die Sozialversicherung
SGB VII	Sozialgesetzbuch VII – Gesetzliche Unfallversicherung
TzBfG	Teilzeitbefristungsgesetz
VAT	value added tax
ZAV	Zentrale Auslands- und Fachvermittlung

Glossary

Act Governing Standard Business Conditions	Recht der Allgemeinen Geschäftsbedingungen
Act on Notification of Conditions Concerning Employment Relationship	Nachweisgesetz
Act on Part-time and Fixed-term Employment	Teilzeit- und Befristungsgesetz
anti-competition clause	Wettbewerbsverbot
application for employment	Bewerbung
arbitration board	Schiedsstelle
balance of interests	Interessenausgleich
benefits	Vergünstigungen; Sozialleistungen
blocking period	Sperrzeit
bonus	Gratifikation
business trip	Dienstreise
cancellation agreement decision	Vergleich
Central Federal Vehicle Registration Authority	Kraftfahrtbundesamt
Central Placement Office of Federal Employment Agency	Zentrale Auslands- und Fachvermittlung
certificate of authority	Vollmacht
certificate of good behavior	Führungszeugnis
certificate of good health	Gesundheitszeugnis (coll.)
certificate of inability to work	Arbeitsunfähigkeitsbescheinigung
Civil Code	Bürgerliches Gesetzbuch
Co-determination Act	Mitbestimmungsgesetz
collective bargaining agreement	Tarifvertrag
Collective Bargaining Agreement Act	Tarifvertragsgesetz
Commercial Code	Handelsgesetzbuch
(commercial) leasing of employees	Arbeitnehmerüberlassung
committee of economic policy	Wirtschaftsausschuss

community involvement	Bürgerschaftliches Engagement
company car	Dienstwagen
company custom	betriebliche Übung
company housing	Dienstwohnung
company secret	Betriebsgeheimnis
company-run daycare center	Betriebskindergarten
compensation for observing competitive restriction	Karenzentschädigung
Confederation of German Trade Unions	Deutscher Gewerkschaftsbund (DGB)
Continued Payment of Wages and Salaries Act	Entgeltfortzahlungsgesetz
continuing effect	Nachwirkung
contract staffing	Arbeitnehmerüberlassung
contract-finalizing agreement	Abwicklungsvertrag
credit bureau	SCHUFA-Auskunft
Data Protection Act	Bundesdatenschutzgesetz
declaration of general application	Allgemeinverbindlichkeitserklärung
deferred compensation	Entgeltumwandlung
diploma from German secondary school qualifying for university admission or matriculation	Abitur
disciplinary warning	Abmahnung
dismissal	Kündigung
dismissal due to operational reasons	betriebsbedingte Kündigung
dismissal for reasons of conduct	verhaltensbedingte Kündigung
dismissal on grounds of personal capability	personenbedingte Kündigung
duty of fidelity	Treuepflicht
duty to provide health care and benefits	Fürsorgepflicht
employee	Arbeitnehmer
employee assignment agreement	Entsendungsvertrag

employee leasing agreement	Arbeitnehmerüberlassungsvertrag
employee liability	Arbeitnehmerhaftung
employee participation program	Mitarbeiterbeteiligungsprogramm
Employee Posting Act	Arbeitnehmerentsendegesetz
employer	Arbeitgeber
employer loans	Arbeitgeberdarlehen
employment contract	Arbeitsvertrag
Employment Protection Act	Kündigungsschutzgesetz
excess hours	Mehrarbeitszeit
extraordinary dismissal	außerordentliche Kündigung
Federal Employment Agency	Bundesagentur für Arbeit
Federal Foreign Office	Auswärtiges Amt
Federal Labor Court	Bundesarbeitsgericht
Federal Leave Act	Bundesurlaubsgesetz
Federal Statistical Office	Statistisches Bundesamt
fictional permanent establishment	Betriebsstättenfiktion
flextime	Vertrauensarbeitszeit
Foreigners` Registration Office	Ausländerbehörde
freedom of association	Koalitionsfreiheit
freelancer	Selbstständiger; Freiberufler
General Equal Treatment Act	Allgemeines Gleichbehandlungsgesetz
General Terms and Conditions	Allgemeine Geschäftsbedingungen
German Civil Service Federation	Deutscher Beamtenbund (dbb)
group works council	Konzernbetriebsrat
hardship allowance	Erschwerniszulage
honorary office	Ehrenamt
human resources	Personal(-abteilung)
immediate dismissal	außerordentliche Kündigung
income replacement benefit	Lohnersatzzahlung
income tax certificate	Lohnsteuerbescheinigung

Industrial Code	Gewerbeordnung
industrial principle	Industrieprinzip
industry-wide collective labor agreement (union)	Verbandstarifvertrag
industry-wide framework/collective agreement	Manteltarifvertrag
Infection Protection Act	Infektionsschutzgesetz
integration office	Integrationsbüro
interim performance review	Zwischenzeugnis
intern	Praktikant; Volontär
internship	Praktikum
internal agreement	Regelungsabrede
job advertisement	Stellenanzeige
job application	Bewerbungsschreiben
job interview	Bewerbungsgespräch
joint works council	Gesamtbetriebsrat
labor dispute	Arbeitskampf
labor union	Gewerkschaft
Law on Parental Allowance and Parental Leave	Gesetz zum Elterngeld und zur Elternzeit
Law regulating the governing standard business conditions	Gesetz zur Regelung des Rechts der Allgemeinen Geschäftsbedingungen
layoff plan (with consideration of social impact)	Sozialplan
leasing of employees	Arbeitnehmerüberlassung
leave of absence/release/leave	Freistellung
legal counsel	Rechtsbeistand
legal guardian	gesetzlicher Vormund
limit of liability	Haftungsbeschränkung
litigation for wrongful termination	Kündigungsschutzprozess
Long-term resident's permit	langfristige Aufenthaltsberechtigung
mass layoffs	Massenentlassung

moonlighting	Mehrfachbeschäftigung
motherhood allowance	Mutterschaftsgeld
National Federation of Christian Trade Unions	Christlicher Gewerkschaftsbund Deutschlands (CGB)
non-disclosure agreement	Geheimhaltungsvertrag
notice period	Kündigungsfrist
Occupational Health and Safety Act	Arbeitsschutzgesetz
Office for Equal Employment Opportunity	Integrationsamt
Office Responsible for Education Allowances	Erziehungsgeldstelle
old-age pension provision	Altersversorgung
on-demand employment relationship	Abrufarbeitsverhältnis
One-third Employee Representation (participation) Act	Drittelbeteiligungsgesetz
opening clause	Öffnungsklausel
Ordinance on Placement of Visual Display Units	Bildschirmarbeitsverordnung
ordinary dismissal	ordentliche Kündigung
overtime	Überstunden
Patent and Trademark Office	Patent- und Markenamt
parental-leave allowance	Elterngeld
partial employment compensation	Kurzarbeitergeld
participatory rights	Mitwirkungsrecht
payroll office	Lohnstelle
penalty clause	Vertragsstrafe
permanent establishment	Betriebsstätte
permanent residence permit	Daueraufenthaltsberechtigung
permission to remain	Aufenthaltsgestattung
personnel file	Personalakte
poaching	abwerben

post-contractual non-compete agreement	nachvertragliches Wettbewerbsverbot
posting employees at other group companies	Konzernversetzung
posting of employees	Entsendungen/Arbeitnehmerentsendung
preclusion period	Ausschlussfrist
principle of good faith	Grundsatz von Treu und Glauben
principle of good morals	Grundsatz der guten Sitten
probationary period	Probezeit
proxy	Bevollmächtigter
public sector	Öffentlicher Dienst
readiness to work	Arbeitsbereitschaft
reference	Zeugnis
reference letter	Arbeitszeugnis
reference provision	Bezugnahmeklausel
representative business establishment	Vertreterbetriebsstätte
representative committee of executive employees	Sprecherausschuss
Residence Act	Aufenthaltsgesetz
residency permit	Aufenthaltserlaubnis, Aufenthaltsgenehmigung
residency permit that allows for employment	Aufenthaltserlaubnis/Aufenthaltsgenehmigung, die zur Erwerbstätigkeit berechtigt
right to consult	Unterrichtungsrecht
risk of liability	Haftungsrisiko
secondary employment	Nebenbeschäftigung
self-employed	Selbstständiger
settlement clause	Abgeltungsklausel
settlement permit	Niederlassungserlaubnis
severance agreement	Aufhebungsvertrag
severance pay	Abfindung
shareholder resolution	Gesellschafterbeschluss
shift work	Schichtarbeit

short-term/low-wage job in which the worker earns under 450 € per month	Minijob
sick pay	Krankengeld
Social Security Code	Sozialgesetzbuch
state pension insurance	gesetzliche Rentenversicherung
stay permit	Aufenthaltstitel
strike	Streik
strike ban	Streikverbot
Tax Code	Abgabenordnung
telecommuting	Telearbeit
Temporary Employment Act	Arbeitnehmerüberlassungsgesetz
temporary suspension of deportation	Duldung
temporary work	Zeitarbeit
termination agreement	Aufhebungsvertrag
termination letter	Kündigungsschreiben
time-credit account	Arbeitszeitkonto
trainee	Auszubildender (aka Azubi)
transfer/posting of employees	Versetzung
under the threshold for full payment of social benefits, on a sliding social security contribution scale, these jobs include those with earnings between 450.01 and 850 €	Midijob
union/trade union	Gewerkschaft
unsolicited application	Initiativbewerbung
unrestricted free movement of workers	Arbeitnehmerfreizügigkeit
vacation allowance	Urlaubsgeld
visa	Visum
vocational training	Berufsausbildung
Vocational Training Act	Berufsbildungsgesetz

wages	Gehalt
work equipment	Betriebsmittel
work-related accident	Arbeitsunfall
Working Hours Act	Arbeitszeitgesetz
working papers	Arbeitspapiere
works agreement	Betriebsvereinbarung
works committee	Betriebsausschuss
Works Constitution Act	Betriebsverfassungsgesetz
Working Times Protection Act	Arbeitszeitgesetz
works council	Betriebsrat
Youth Employment Protection Act	Jugendarbeitsschutzgesetz

Part 1
Introduction to German Employment Law

I. German Employment Market – Stats and Facts

1. German Employment by the Numbers

In 2012, 41,586,000 people were employed in Germany, and the **majority of them were employed full-time**. In 2012 there were 29,413,605 employees responsible for paying social insurance contributions and 7,386,881 of them were under-employed.[1] For 2011 there were 29,980,000 people with a **permanent employment contract** (of which 15,632,000 were male and 14,258,000 female) and 5,186,000 with a **fixed-term employment contract**; 25,716,000 worked full-time and 9,512,000 part-time.[2] At that time the **unemployment rate** stood at approximately 6.8%, which worked out to 2,397,000 unemployed people of working age.[3] The real gross domestic product for 2012 grew only about 0.7% and amounted to 2.645 Billion €; a year earlier, in 2011, that amount was +3%. 1

Real wages, that is, the gross monthly income after adjustments for inflation, 2
increased in Germany in 2012 by an average of 0.5% from the previous year. Looking at the actual numbers, the average gross monthly wage in 2012 stood at 3,391 €.[4] In the **eastern part of Germany**, however, one sees a lower average monthly – and thus annual – wage than that of the western part of the country. Further, a considerable number of unskilled workers earn less than this in both the east and west. That said, skilled workers can earn quite a bit more.

It is further worth noting that claims for **partial-employment compensation** 3
increased. In July 2012, 54,000 people received partial-employment compensation.[5] However, one must keep in mind: these numbers are not set in stone, as they depend on numerous factors and therefore merely provide a rough idea.

---

1 Employment statistics, German Federal Employment Agency ("Bundesagentur für Arbeit"), date of reference: June 30, 2012 (http://www.arbeitsagentur.de).

2 Statistics from the German Federal Statistical Office ("Statistisches Bundesamt"), year of reference: 2011 (http://www.destatis.de).

3 Employment statistics, German Federal Employment Agency ("Bundesagentur für Arbeit"), date of reference: May 28, 2013 (http://www.arbeitsagentur.de).

4 Average gross monthly wages statistics, 2012 (http://www.statista.de).

5 Employment statistics, German Federal Employment Agency ("Bundesagentur für Arbeit"), Monthly Report, January 2013 (http://www.arbeitsagentur.de).

2. Flexible Types of Employment

4 According to the numbers **employment contracts of indefinite duration** statistically represent the most common form of employment in Germany. However, factors such as demographic shifts, financial crises, globalization and of course the change in employee expectations and needs have created a changed working world, one that cannot function only with rigid regulations. By way of the so-called **atypical employment model** ("atypische Beschäftigungsmodelle") – which is a full-time employment relationship that is not indefinite in duration – companies have the ability to flexibly react to changes in given employment relationships and thereby satisfy market demands.

a) On-demand Work

5 In certain business sectors there are **periodic increases in workload.** Employers often wish that they could fit the working hours of their employees to the actual demands for work and flexibly set up the working hours in such situations.

6 As a rule, on-demand work relationships are **permanent employment relationships** in Germany. Of advantage for the employer is the fact that he/she does not have to continually train new people. Economically speaking, it is especially advantageous for the employer that the individual working hours are not linked to traditional hours of operation. Instead they are determined by the actual work needs.

7 The advantage employees enjoy as a result of these agreements is that they can rely on a continuous income even during periods when demands for work are low. With regard to the **scope of minimum working hours**, the contractual parties are, as far as German employment laws are concerned, free to negotiate as they see fit. Should there be no minimum working hours established per contract, the employer has to utilize the services of the employee for at least three consecutive hours after calling upon him/her to work.

b) Employee Leasing ("Arbeitnehmerüberlassung")

8 With employee leasing, the employer (leaser) loans his/her employee (temporary employee) to a third party (contracting party) to perform work. However, the **employment relationship** is between the leaser and employee. Between the leaser and the contracting party, there is a **transfer agreement.** No contractual relationship actually exists between the (temporary) employee and the contracting party. The leaser's right to instruct employees will, within the framework of the employee transfer agreement, be carried over to the contracting party.

9 Employee leasing represents an employment model that has been steadily growing in Germany, with the number of leased employees in Germany doubling since

2005. This is above all else due to the fact that leased employees, by way of **temporary work**, can end their existing unemployment situation, or gain work experience by working as a leased employee and obtain a chance to get a permanent position. The contracting party has the benefit of being able to react flexibly to varying market demands by using leased, temporary workers without having to bind him-/herself to a given employee for a longer period of time. The legal principles for employee leasing in Germany are found in the **Temporary Employment Act** ("Arbeitnehmerüberlassungsgesetz – AÜG"). The hiring out of employees requires an appropriate authorization from the leaser from the German Employment Agency for that given jurisdiction.

c) Fixed-term Employment

Nearly every second new hire in Germany is working under a fixed-term agreement. 10
Fixed-term employment is an employment relationship with a **specific duration** that ends on a specific date or with a specific result so that a **notice of termination** is not required. It is, in a manner of speaking, a separate case for termination. For these employment contracts, the German **Part-Time Work and Temporary Employment Contracts Act** ("Teilzeit- und Befristungsgesetz – TzBfG") applies. The negotiated fixed-term of employment has to be in writing.

d) "One-Euro" Workers

The opportunity to work in a so-called "One-Euro" job exists in Germany. This 11
means that employable persons receiving state aid and who are **receiving unemployment benefits** ("Arbeitslosengeld II") can, by way of an employment opportunity, earn additional money and experience. Similar to the welfare-to-work program in the United States, the aim of this measure is to lead long-term unemployed back into the regular job market, from one Euro per hour to full-time employment, as it were. When establishing the legal basis, it is important not to create an employment relationship in the traditional German sense. Rather, the person working a "One-Euro" job has a legal relationship that is far more **shaped by public law**. It is therefore only fitting that the prerequisites for "One-Euro" jobs are that

- there is a need,
- the work continues to increase,
- it is in the public interest, and
- is competition-neutral.

In practice all local public and non-profit companies therefore come to mind with 12
"One-Euro" jobs.

e) Minijob workers

13 The model for **marginal employment** in Germany, the so-called “minijob”, has become an important form of employment, with 7.5 million people currently working in such a job. The term minijob refers to low-wage employment and other short-term employment. Marginal employment is **shaped principally by German Social Security Law**, because the worker is, according to this law, in an employment relationship that is largely not subject to social insurance. There are, however, exceptions with respect to state pension insurance contributions for marginal wage jobs.

14 The same employment law regulations apply to minijobs as those for more traditional employment relationships. For example, someone working a minijob is **entitled to advance payment** in case of illness, as well as a right to vacation time as set forth by the German Federal Leave Act (“Bundesurlaubsgesetz – BUrlG”). The legal foundation is the German Social Security Code, Book IV (“Sozialgesetzbuch IV – SGB IV”).

15 The recently raised **wage limit** for mini jobs is now at 450 € per month.

3. Social Security System and the 50/50 Split

16 There are four **key elements** to the German social security system and along with these come several smaller ones. The key ones are:

- unemployment insurance,
- health insurance,
- disability insurance, and
- pension insurance.

17 Based on gross salary, monthly premiums range from 1.95% for disability health to the high of 19.6% for retirement insurance in 2012. The cost is principally divided in half, with the employer paying the one half and the employee the other, a **50/50 split**. A few exceptions do exist, however. German regulations mandate, what appears at least on the surface, a rather sensible exception for employees without children. They are required to pay an extra 25% for their disability insurance premium. One of the reasons is that, since they do not have children to care for them later, the state may very well have to. Another exception from the 50/50 split may be found in the premiums for health insurance. Employers pay 7.3% of these premiums while the employees contribute 8.2%. For **employees with children**, all of these social insurance contributions work out to 40.05% of their respective gross salaries, with the number coming to 40.3% for employees who are childless. Please note, however, that these contributions are capped and stop at a certain salary level.

4. Annual paid leave

Work weeks vary by industry sector and by location, but mostly range between **37 and 40 hours weekly**. The legal minimum paid holiday entitlement is 20 work days per annum for employees working a five-day week. Depending on how many days per week the employee has to work, it can be calculated using this formula: 18

24 workdays × number of work days per week / 6 employee vacation days

Workdays per Week	Vacation Days per Year
6	24
5	20
4	16
3	12
2	8
1	4

Collective bargaining and trade union and other employment agreements often increase this, with most entitlements to vacation ranging between 25 and 30 days per annum. It should be noted that management and older employees are often entitled to as many as 32 days of vacation time per annum. Additionally, **handicapped people** are entitled to additional paid vacation time of one work week. 19

Along with this **teens** have a right to more vacation time than adults. The legal minimum of vacation days for teens who have not reached their 16th birthday by the beginning of the given calendar year is 30 workdays; for teens who have not reached their 17th birthday who by the beginning of the given calendar year is 27 workdays; and for teens who have not reached their 18th birthday by the beginning of the given calendar year is 25 workdays. 20

Public and other holidays vary from 10 to 13 days annually depending on which of the 16 German states, or “Länder”, one is speaking about. 21

If the employee is prevented from working for reasons that are no fault of his own, **additional paid leave** may be granted to him/her in special cases (death, wedding, birth). The legal entitlement to extra paid leave can be amended or precluded by an individual employment contract, a works agreement or a collective bargaining agreement. For example, additional leave of three days may be granted for the death of a spouse. Further, additional, **unpaid leave** can be taken for certain circumstances (e.g. when the employee’s child is ill). 22

In cases of **illnesses** that are no fault of the employee, he/she retains a right to salary for the time he/she is out, up to six weeks. The employee is obliged to inform the employer of his/her inability to work. Should the absence from work exceed three days, the employer has to provide the employer with a **doctor’s note** no later 23 than the next workday. The legal basis for this is the entitlement to German law on continued remuneration.

II. Specifics of German Employment Law

1. Understanding the Basic Principles

24 German law does not codify employment law in a singular "Employment Act". Instead, one finds employment matters addressed in **several different legislative acts**. The most common paperback treatment covers 60 main, employment-related acts and several others for the layperson's daily use. The more common published laws can be understood to include:

A = "Arbeitszeitgesetz" (Employment law), "Arbeitnehmerüberlassung" (employee transfer);
B = "Bundesurlaubsgesetz" (Federal Leave Act);
D = "Drittelbeteiligungsgesetz" (One-Third Employee Representation (Participation) Act);
E = "Elternzeitgesetz" (Parental Leave Act);
K = "Kündigungsschutzgesetz" (Employment Protection Act);
M = "Mutterschutzgesetz" (Maternity Leave Act);
S = "Sozialgesetzbücher" (Social Security Code);
T = "Teilzeitbefristungsgesetz" (Act on Part-time Work and Fixed-term Employment Relationships), etc.

25 Additionally and, for many familiar with **Roman law traditions**, surprisingly, case law has tremendous impact on German employment law. **Jurisprudence** from the German labor courts – from the German Federal Labor Court in particular – play a major role in patching the holes found in employment-related statutes. In 2010, 559,080 cases were pending before local labor law courts, 39,882 in front of the state courts of appeal and 2,471 in front of the Federal Labor Law Court.[6]

26 As one looks at German employment law regulations, one thing becomes obvious: its principle objective is the **protection of employees** working within the country's borders. The schematic for breaking down how these protections work is best explained as a hierarchical pyramid:

6 Statistics from the Ministry of Labor and Social Affairs, German Federal Statistical Office, specialty series 10, volume 2.8, 2010 (http://www.bmas.de).

As one might imagine, if the issue is located high in the hierarchical pyramid, its jurisprudential significance is correspondingly higher with respect to German employment laws ("Rangprinzip"). As with most things in law, there are exceptions, and the principle of deviating from a given collective bargaining agreement for the employee´s benefit ("Günstigkeitsprinzip") is one in this regard. This principle is simpler than it may sound to non-Germans: that which is **more beneficial to the employee** remains in force, regardless of the level in the hierarchy, as long as the given provision is valid law (note: "Günstigkeit" = favorability). Such deviations from statutory regulations, work agreements or collective bargain agreements that show favor toward employees are nearly always permissible. 27

2. Individual Employment Agreements and Collective Bargaining Agreements

Individual employment agreements between employers and employees represent the **main legal source** regarding employment relationships. It should be noted that it is customary for all employees at all levels to have a signed contract in Germany. To that point, most employers use a **standard employment contract** for all of their employees in order to make their HR process manageable. In any event, these documents are generally governed by the German Act Governing Standard Business Conditions ("Gesetz zur Regelung des Rechts der Allgemeinen Geschäftsbedingungen – AGB-Gesetz"). 28

29 A works agreement ("Betriebsvereinbarung"), on the other hand, represents an agreement between employers and the given works council (definition below). They **regulate work conditions** where no collective bargaining agreement ("Tarifvertrag") exists. Works agreements directly influence employment relationships, since they have an immediate and binding effect on individual employment relationships, as statutory law would. Thus, employers do not have to seek negotiations with each employee. For example, if the given company wants to initiate reduced working hours, it can conclude a works agreement with the works council that affects all the employment relationships for employees that fall within the works agreement's scope.

30 As for the collective bargaining agreement, an employers' association or an individual employer negotiates and concludes a contract with a **trade union**. These types of agreements regulate a sizeable number of crucial working condition matters. A basic collective agreement lays out issues central to the employment relationship, such as the number of hours to be worked weekly, explanation of vacation and leave days, extended termination periods and matters of similar weight. German law does not require employers to sign collective bargain agreements or join employer associations, thus usage of them is not either. An exception will be found in a declaration making the agreement generally binding ("Allgemeinverbindlichkeitserklärung") of a collective labor agreement by legislators. Collective labor agreements that are generally binding establish general standards for application for all employment contracts within such an agreement's scope. This occurs regardless of what collective labor agreement the contracting parties agree upon. Every collective labor agreement concluded in Germany is listed in **tariff registries** that are accessible to the public. The German Federal Department of Labor ("Arbeitsministerium") manages these tariff registry lists and they are available in each German state.

III. Applying Foreign Law in the Light of German Constitutional Rights and Employment Law

31 The German Basic Law ("Grundgesetz"), the country's constitutional document, sets the tone for fair treatment and ethics for German employment relationships. That document's collection of human and citizen rights has a clear **effect on employer-employee relationships**, as its principles are the foundation for principally all law in Germany. If a group of employees wish to join a trade union, they can find their guaranty to freedom of association laid out in the Basic Law. Yes, European law court decisions and legislation is increasingly gaining importance in all EU countries and is therefore having an effect on German employment law. That said, the unique characteristics of the German system remain.

32 German law does not always require its application. Therefore, foreign employees and their employer working at a German location might agree to **apply their own, foreign (non-German) employment laws**. Though this is possible, it is nei-

ther commonplace nor recommendable. Reason: the law governing employment relationships and agreements should not lead to a situation where employees lose security and protection, or other rights German law statutes guarantee.

Here are some **examples**: the application of American law is stipulated in the 33
employment agreement.

Example 1
If a female employee becomes pregnant, not American but German regulations regarding maternity leave would have to be applied for female employees working mainly in Germany.

Example 2
German regulations protecting the employee found in areas concerning maximum working hours would have to be put into force regardless of the given in-house agreement to apply a foreign law's stipulations in this regard. For companies with a works agreement in force, the German Works Constitution Act's principle of territoriality comes into play. A foreign company's office and other establishments in Germany fall within the scope of and are thus subject to the act, so long as the given office qualifies as an individual legal entity and may disregard direction from its foreign headquarters. In such a case, avoiding the need of a works council because it would not be customary in the home country is simply impossible; German law would find application here.

In short, applying foreign law is a trap that one might better avoid. 34

IV. Relationships and Roles in German Employment Law

There are **key relationships** anyone doing business in Germany needs to be aware 35
of:

- The individual relationship between employer and employee. For the most part, it is regulated by individual employment contracts;
- Employers' associations serving the collective interest of employers;
- Employee/employer relations to trade unions;
- Employee and employer relations to works councils;
- Employee and employer regulations in collective bargaining agreements;
- Employee and employer regulations in works agreements.

For clarity's sake, consider now how these individuals and groups are defined.

1. Employees

An employee is an individual who carries out his/her work "dependently" for the 36
benefit of another, an employer. This relationship is based on a **civil law contract**. Criteria for employment and thus working dependently is that the employee:

- has to comply with the employer's directives regarding location, duration and scope of time, the work is to be performed,
- is dependent on the employer both financially and for work in general (as opposed to a self-employed person),
- has to provide services in accordance with the employer's directives in order to receive compensation in return,
- is a clear participant in the employer's organization.

37 The criteria for working sets employees and consultants, freelancers or independent contractors apart, since the latter three groups base their relationship and thus the performance of their services on a **service contract**. Here is the key point: if the services are rendered by someone who is **economically and socially independent** from the employer, the agreement for that work is not an employment agreement but a mere service contract.

38 As in most other countries, an employee can be employed part- or full-time in Germany. An employee is considered to be part-time if the weekly hours worked are less than those worked by comparable full-time employees at the particular company. There are laws in Germany that allow those who work full-time to **apply for part-time work** based on reasons such as parental leave or partial retirement. Consultants, freelancers or independent contractors do not enjoy such a privilege, since they are not technically considered employees and are, rather, seen as being **self-employed** under German law. Also much like other countries, the consultants, freelancers or independent contractors have to pay their own **taxes** while employee's payroll deductions address these kinds of matters automatically. Further, services contracts are not restricted by employment laws, and this allows the contracting parties to settle on contractual stipulations such as pay, period of time the contract lasts, services due as they choose. Also, consultants, freelancers or independent contractors can be summarily dismissed in most cases.

2. Works Councils

39 Elected for a term of four years by their fellow employees, the works council ("Betriebsrat") is the employee representative body in Germany. The **size and existence of a works council** depends largely on the company's size. German law does not compel employees to elect a works council; however, employees have a right to institute a works council in so long as at least five employees are continuously employed there. Of five employees, three would be eligible for election. Legally, employers are forbidden from stopping the establishment of an election for a works council.

40 Employees must form a joint works council ("Gesamtbetriebsrat") if their company is comprised of **multiple establishments**. In this regard, corporate groups can

form a group works council ("Konzernbetriebsrat") in cases when a corporate group has more than one, joint works council. The German Works Constitution Act regulates the rights and duties of works councils, joint works councils and group works councils. This legislative act contains several works council co-determination rights that apply for matters such as measures affecting the business's organizational or operational issues.

3. Unions

Unions are employee associations instituted for the improvement of employee working conditions. Importantly, they are very helpful to employees in concluding collective bargaining agreements. Protected by the German constitution, trade unions are **formed for and by a particular industry**. Currently, over 7 million employees are union members, spread out among 64 different trade unions in Germany. 41

They are broken down by industry to better serve the particular needs of the given industry (i.e. steel, miners, etc.), **irrespective of the job** performed at the given company. For example, this allows for specialists in an office in the steel industry company to be associated with the union for the steel industry. There are also long-standing, specialized unions that often cooperate with larger trade unions in these branches. 42

Currently, approximately 20% of all companies' employees in Germany are organized in unions with about 465 binding collective labor agreements in force. Though there is **not de jure a minimum wage** in Germany, there are nine contracts setting one that is valid for their given industry. On the contrary, about 44% of all employees work in companies without valid collective labor agreements. However, even half of these companies paid wages that generally conform to in force collective labor agreements. Even in "union shops", employees have a choice of whether or not to become members of a trade union. 43

4. Employers' Associations

The counterpart of trade unions are employers' associations whose primary purpose is to negotiate and subsequently conclude **collective bargaining agreements**. As with employees and trade unions, employers are not legally compelled to become a member of any employers' association. 44

Employers' associations or their respective employers negotiate on an equal footing. The two contracting parties negotiate on collective labor agreements that pertain to all employees in their given companies or industries. The German **government only regulates the framework** for negotiations. 45

46 An **employer's withdrawal** from its particular employers' association with which an industry-wide collective labor agreement ("Verbandstarifvertrag") was negotiated does not stop the tariff commitment immediately. Rather, the departing employer and given trade union **remain bound to the collective labor agreement** until the time when the collective labor agreement ends due to the employers' association's or the union's termination. Once the collective labor agreement expires, it remains in force until a new understanding is arrived at, which effectively means that any working conditions agreed upon in the recently expired collective labor agreement are valid for the respectively affected employment contracts. A **new understanding** could be placed in either a new collective labor agreement or in a change of the standard employment contract. This continuing effect ("Nachwirkung") only impacts those employees who were already employed when the term of the collective labor agreement expired or who are members of the respective labor union.

5. Supervisory board

47 As part of the corporate governance, a supervisory board – which may also be construed to refer to a board of directors – is required:
- to oversee how the company management operates and
- to appoint and to terminate the managing directors as appropriate.

48 What may seem surprising to those not familiar with German employment law is that **employees have a right of co-determination** in this regard, but this is qualified by under the following conditions. Pursuant to the German One-Third Employee Representation (Participation) Act ("Drittelbeteiligungsgesetz"), publically owned corporations ("AG"), partnerships limited by shares ("KGaA") and, under certain conditions, limited liability companies ("GmbH") with more than 500 employees, one-third of the supervisory board membership has to be employee representatives directly elected by employees. If the company in question regularly employs more than 2,000 employees, the German Co-determination Act ("Mitbestimmungsgesetz") applies. Under this Co-determination Act **supervisory boards** are required to have a membership comprised of an equal shareholder and employee representation.

Part 2
618 Frequently Asked Questions

Chapter 1 Age | Alter

Definition, Legal Principles[7]

!

The age of those entering and leaving the workforce is **legislatively regulated**, the reason being that children and teens should and do enjoy special protection in order to ensure that their schooling and development are not negatively impacted by other forms of work. Generally speaking, a child of 13 may work in more minor jobs, such as being a newspaper carrier. Teenagers – those who are already 15 but who have not yet reached 18 years of age – may work up to 40 hours per week.

In the context of continuing education, **younger workers** have the possibility of working as a student worker, intern, trainee, or student apprentice. The primary difference between this and a fixed employment relationship is that such an arrangement serves the primary objective of educating younger workers. With a view to possibly working in a company under a temporary agreement, younger workers are given the chance to become acquainted with different organizations, make contacts and come to learn their own strengths at an early stage in their respective careers.

For **older employees** (those who are 55 or older), the possibility of smooth transition from working life into retirement exists within the framework of a **partial retirement plan** with the reduction of working hours. The retirement age in Germany currently lies between 65 and 67 years of age, with the precise date determined by one's month and year of birth (see the answer to the second question and answer in this section for more). Further, the opportunity to voluntarily enter into early retirement exists, but it is tied to reductions in retirement pay. The decisive role age plays in direct and indirect disadvantage comes into play within the framework of the General Act on Equal Treatment ("Allgemeines Gleichbehandlungsgesetz – AGG"). No employee may be discriminated against due to age via the conditions of employment, vocational training, social protection, etc. It should be noted that, in Germany during the last few years, more than 56% of all of those employed are between 55 and 65 years old.

Question 1
When does an employee have to retire due to age?

Answer
In Germany there is no legally determined maximum age. With nearly all German 1
employment contracts and collective bargaining agreements, the employment relationship ends when the employee reaches **retirement age** or is **permanently unable to work** any longer.

7 For further information about the retirement plan, see Chapter 28.

Question 2
What is the retirement age in Germany?

Answer
2 The statutory retirement age lies currently between 65 and 67 years of age. The concrete retirement age within this range **depends on the year of birth**. Beginning on January 1, 2012 German law required people wishing to retire to work one year longer than they had before. That means that an employee born in 1947 was able to retire in 2012 at age 65 and one month. This scale increases until, for those born in 1958, the employee has to work an extra year, meaning that he or she will be able to enter into regular retirement at age 66 in 2024. Between 2024 and 2029, **the increase is two months per year**, ultimately ending in 2029 with any employee born in 1964 – or later – not being able to enter into regular retirement until age 67 without getting reduced retirement payments.

Question 3
May an older employee work few hours and only partially retire?

Answer
3 Yes, an older employee can make a claim for partial retirement. The partial retirement agreement represents a **fully valid employment relationship**. The hours can be evenly **reduced in half** for the entire time or an **uneven distribution** of hours worked can be agreed upon. For this the conclusion of an appropriate employment contract is required.

Question 4
Can minors – those older than 7 and under 18 years of age – also be employees?

Answer
4 Yes. However, a minor requires the **permission of a legal representative** (parent or legal guardian) before concluding an employment contract. If the minor concludes the employment contract without the required permission, the enforceability of the contract depends on the authorization of the legal representative. If this condition is not met, the employment contract is unenforceable. Options in accordance with collective bargaining agreement are to be regarded as customary. Further, a minor is entitled to **announce a termination** notice without the presence of the legal representative and to receive it. Additionally, the German Youth Employment Protection Act ("Jugendarbeitsschutzgesetz – JArbSchG") contains proscriptions and limitations on minors working.

Question 5

How does the legal invalidity of an employment agreement between a minor and an employee have influence on an employee who is a minor?

Answer

If the employment relationship comes into effect without the permission of a legal 5
representative, a what is known in German Employment Law as **de facto employment relationship** exists. It can be immediately ended via a unilateral statement without the pre-condition of an extraordinary notice of dismissal existing. For the time already elapsed, the minor retains his right to remuneration as well as various other rights, such as vacation time/overtime payment, bonus etc.

Chapter 2 Anti-Competition Clause | Wettbewerbsverbot

Definition, Legal Principles
A contractual anti-competition clause signifies that every competitive activity during the legal existence of an employee's employment relationship with a given employer that disadvantages that employer is forbidden. Formally speaking, this comes from the German Civil Code, sec. 241, para. 2, which stipulates a duty of fidelity the employee has, and this duty is to be taken into consideration with respect to the rights, objects of legal protection and interests of the contractual partners. Beyond the anti-competition clause set out in the contract, German law acknowledges a **post-contractual anti-competition ban**, which indicates that the employee is also contractually bound after the employment relationship has ended not to engage in competition against the former employer. What must indeed kept in mind, however, is that such an agreement only has a **maximum duration of up to two years**, and the former employee is **entitled to compensation** for observing competitive restriction.

Question 6
What is an anti-competition clause from a German Employment Law perspective?

Answer

1 An anti-competition clause refers to the limitation of the given commercial activity with consideration of an existing or prior employment relationship. The anti-competition clause prohibits the employee from **engaging in a forbidden competitive endeavor**. Engaging in a competitive business exists, for example, when the employee poaches another employee for the purpose of building his/her own rival firm or loan a competitor a sizeable amount of money.

Question 7
What are the legal consequences might one suffer for violating an anti-competition clause?

Answer

2 The employer can be provided with justification for ordinary or even extraordinary dismissal due to the impermissible competition.[1] He can also adhere to the contract and oblige the employee to desist. Further, the employee makes him/herself **liable for damages**. So long as the anti-competition clause was violated during the time of employment, the employer **can demand profits** gained from the employee's com-

1 Federal Labor Court ("Bundesarbeitsgericht – BAG"), ruling dated November 21, 1996 – 2 AZR 852/95 –.

petitive business activities as damages. In such an instance it must be proven that the employee carried out the prohibited competitive business activities on his own (sec. 61 para. 1 German Commercial Code – "§ 61 Abs. 1 HGB"). Should the employee violate a **post-contractual non-compete agreement**, the employer is automatically freed from the obligation of having to pay a compensation for observing competitive restriction for the duration of the violation of the anti-competition clause. Further, the employer has a right to be informed, injunctive relief and a claim for damages.

Question 8

May an employee work for another employer despite a non-compete agreement?

Answer

Employees may not perform for others or as a self-employed person a job in the 3
same field of business activity as the current employer. There is an exception if consent from the given employer has been granted, e.g. for secondary employment or multiple job holdings (**moonlighting**).

Question 9

Would a German anti-competition clause allow an employee to work in a self-employed capacity during his employment relationship with the employer he/she has made the agreement with?

Answer

Only with the consent of the employer may an employee work in a self-employed 4
capacity during his existing employment relationship.

Question 10

Is the poaching/headhunting of employees permissible in a German anti-competition clause?

Answer

The poaching of workers external to the given company is a part of free competition 5
and, as a rule, is permissible. It is, then, **anti-competitive** if a competitive relationship exists between the company doing the poaching and the one being poached from. In this respect, poaching is anti-competitive if unfair concomitant circumstances are added, especially if unfair means are applied or unfair purposes are pursued.

Question 11
May an employee work at a competitor company after the given employment relationship with the former employer has ended?

Answer
6 As a rule, anti-competition clauses end at the conclusion of the employment relationship. However, even after the end of the employment relationship the former employee and employer can sign an agreement that forbids competition, a **post-contractual non-compete agreement** ("nachvertragliches Wettbewerbsverbot").

Question 12
What does German Employment Law understand compensation for observing competitive restriction ("Karenzentschädigung") to be?

Answer
7 The compensation for observing competitive restriction represents compensation for **losses incurred by a post-contractual non-compete agreement.** At the same time it is a prerequisite for the validity of the anti-competition clause. The amount must have a value of at least 50% of the employee's entire compensation (i.e. including bonuses, company car, etc.). The payment takes place pro rata temporis.

Question 13
What are the consequences if the employer pays the (former) employee compensation for observing competitive restriction?

Answer
8 If it becomes evident that a **lower compensation** for observing competitive restriction has been paid, i.e. the employer pays only 20% of the last salary received by the (former) employee, the employee cannot be held liable should he/she choose to ignore the anti-competition clause.

Question 14
For how long of a period does a post-contractual non-compete agreement last?

Answer
9 A post-contractual non-compete agreement may only stipulate that it be adhered to for **two years or less** after the end of the employment relationship. A commitment of more than two years would represent an impermissible disadvantage of the employee and would therefore be invalid under German law.

Question 15
Can employers and employees rescind a post-contractual non-compete agreement?

Answer
Yes, an anti-competition clause can be rescinded by mutual consent in writing be- 10
fore and after the end of the employment relationship.

Question 16
Can the employer waive an anti-competition ban?

Answer
The employer can waive an anti-competition ban before the end of the employment 11
relationship. If done, the employer has to **explain the waiver in writing**. He/she can put the waiver in connection with a letter of dismissal or a severance agreement.

Question 17
Is the agreement on contractual penalties for anti-competition clause violations permissible?

Answer
Yes, the employer can stipulate that there is a penalty clause for the event that the 12
employee violates the anti-competition clause. This stipulation has to be **in written form**.

Chapter 3 Application for Employment | Bewerbung

Definition, Legal Principles

Along with applying for a posted job vacancy, there is always the possibility of sending an unsolicited application. By way of an interview and related negotiations connected to a possible employment relationship, there is a legal obligation with reciprocal duty to proper care. This **pre-contractual obligation** exists without consideration whether the employment relationship materializes or not. In fact, if the obligations have been violated, there can be claims to damages. For this reason, documentation and archiving of application procedures is required.

Of note is the fact that the German General Act on Equal Treatment has considerable effects on **application procedures**. For example, **unequal treatment** on the basis of one's personal characteristics is forbidden. Any job announcement has to be carefully formulated and has to be vetted for possibly impermissible criteria.

Lastly, if an employee is looking for a new job after he/she has been terminated, the employer has to allow the employee leave from work for an adequate period of time to look for a new job.

Question 18

What information needs to be included in a job advertisement?

Answer

1 A job advertisement in Germany has to include the following information about the job:

- responsibilities,
- skills,
- key requirements,
- skill level.

Question 19

What are the laws on non-discrimination in Germany?

Answer

2 The German General Equal Treatment Act ("Allgemeines Gleichbehandlungsgesetz – AGG") prohibits discrimination based on race, ethnicity, gender, religion or (secular) belief, disability, and sexual identity. There is **no quota** in Germany. This has influence an all aspects of an employment relationship: hiring process, remuneration, promotion, dismissals, etc.

Question 20

What is included in a standard German job application?

Answer

Included are 3
- a letter of application,
- CV/resume with photo,
- references and certificates from former employers,
- school and college transcripts,
- certificates of vocational training, and
- reference letters.

Historically, a photograph is normally included in an employment application 4
package. Currently, there is no law explicitly forbidding employers from requiring one in Germany. But, employers must be aware that the photograph allows conclusions to be drawn and could be used against the employer later should the applicant file a discrimination claim.

Question 21

May the employer forward the application materials at its disposal to others within the firm?

Answer

The employer may not make anyone's application materials **widely available.** On 5
the other hand, an exception can be made for someone who has reason to look at the application materials, e.g. works council.

Question 22

May the employer forward the application materials at its disposal to others outside the firm?

Answer

This is not generally allowed. If the employer allows him/herself to be advised by a 6
consulting service provider or selects an outside firm for its hiring purposes, the application materials may be forwarded in so far as that they are not already in possession of the documentation.

Question 23

How may the application materials be saved?

Answer

7 There is neither a statute nor a German Federal Labor Court decision on the matter. If a rejected applicant files a General Act on Equal Treatment complaint ("AGG-Klage"), the employer is required to demonstrate that all applicants were handled equally. For this reason it makes sense for the employer to keep the **3-year statute of limitations** in mind.

Question 24

May an applicant's information be saved for an applicant pool?

Answer

8 The saving of this information is only allowed if the applicant is notified and his/her permission is given.

Question 25

Who covers the costs of gathering and producing the application materials?

Answer

9 The employee covers these costs. Some typical examples include photocopies, photos and driver's license.

Question 26

Do the application materials need to be returned to the applicant at the end of the application process?

Answer

10 No, as there is no obligation to return the materials. However, the employer has to give the applicant the possibility to get those application materials back. They **remain the property of the applicant** and may not be destroyed without his/her permission.

Question 27

Does the rejection of an applicant have to be in writing?

Answer

11 No, the rejection, for example, can also be oral or in electronic form (i.e. e-mail).

Question 28
Do there need to be reasons for rejecting a candidate?

Answer
No, the person rejected for a given position has no right to information about why he/she did not get the position or who was ultimately hired. One exception that would make sharing this information necessary, however, would be those cases where there is a **danger of discrimination.** 12

Question 29
Does the works council need to be informed about the candidate hired?

Answer
Yes, the employer has to participate with the works council in personnel matters by law. This means the works council has to **be informed** before the employment contract has been signed. The employer has to provide so-called required documents for a proper participation. "Required documents" include those documents submitted by the applicant and those the employer created during the application process (e.g. employee-produced application form). 13

Question 30
Can the works council oppose hiring a particular candidate?

Answer
Yes, the works council can oppose a staffing decision. In such a case, the employer would be **forbidden from carrying out** that decision. However, the employer can have a labor court's decision replace the approved of the works council. As stated in the Works Constitution Act, an interim injunction is possible: 14

> **"Section 100**
> **Temporary staff movements**
> *(1) The employer may, if this is urgently required for reasons based on facts, make a staff movement within the meaning of the first sentence of section 99 (1) on a temporary basis before the works council takes a stand or if it has refused its consent. In such cases the employer shall inform the employee concerned of the position in fact and in law.*
> *(2) The employer shall immediately notify the works council of the temporary staff movement. If the works council contends the urgency of the action taken on grounds based on facts, it shall immediately report its objection to the employer. In such cases the employer shall be allowed to maintain the temporary staff movement only on condition that within three days he applies to the labor court for a decision in lieu of the consent of the works council and for a declaration stating that the action taken was urgently required for reasons based on facts.*

(3) If the labor court by mandatory decision refuses to issue a decision in lieu of the works council's consent or if it hands down a final mandatory judgment to the effect that the action taken was manifestly not urgently required by reasons based on facts, the temporary staff movement shall be cancelled on the expiry of two weeks after the date on which the decision or judgment becomes operative. After that date it shall be unlawful to maintain the staff movement."[1]

Question 31
Does the works council need to take part in the interviewing process?

Answer
15 No. According to the German Federal Labor Court, the works council has no right to participate in interviewing candidates. However, a works agreement might state that the works council can be conceded rights to participate in the interview or discussions related to it.

Question 32
Does the employer have to pay for the applicant's costs for travel to the interview?[2]

Answer
16 Yes, except if the payment of certain costs are excluded in the interview invitation.

Question 33
Does the employer have to assume the employee's moving costs?

Answer
17 No, as there is no legally recognized entitlement to moving cost compensation. However, some employers in Germany do offer to assume or contribute to the costs of moving.

Question 34
Does that apply to an unsolicited application?

---

1 Source: German Ministry of Justice (http://www.gesetze-im-internet.de/englisch_betrvg/englisch_betrvg.html).

2 See also Chapter 13.

Answer

Employers need not react to unsolicited applications. They do not even have to return the application materials. The only time this would apply would be when the applicant supplied a **return envelope** with sufficient postage on it. 18

Chapter 4 Collective Bargaining Agreement | Tarifvertrag

! **Definition, Legal Principles**

In total there are about 68,000 collective bargaining agreements in Germany.[1] Of these about 10,000 were **company agreements** in 2011.[2] The percentage of people bound by collective bargaining agreements in 2010 was 63% in the western and 50% in the eastern parts of Germany, respectively.[3]

A collective bargaining agreement is a **written contract** between an employers' association or individual company and a worker's union in which the rights and obligations of the contractual parties are fixed. The collective bargaining agreement contains German legal standards that can regulate the content, the conclusion and the termination of employment relationships as well as corporate issues and issues under the German Works Constitution Act.

There is a differentiation made between industry-wide collective agreements (relates to vacation, working hours, probationary periods, notice periods and shift-work regulations), sectoral or centralized collective agreements (applies to a specific region, usually a state), collective wage agreements (which regulate the amount of remuneration for work performed by the employee, Christmas bonuses and vacation money) and company-wide collective agreements (collective agreements that are solely between the local union and the given company). The legal norm for collective bargaining agreements have **direct and compulsory effect** and can also be valid after the collective agreement's agreed upon end date.

Question 35

What is a collective bargaining agreement understood to be under German law?

Answer

1 A collective bargaining agreement is a contract between two contractual partners. It is regulated by the German Collective Bargaining Agreement Act ("Tarifvertragsgesetz").

Question 36

Who may conclude a collective bargaining agreement?

---

1 According to the Federal Ministry of Labor and Social Affairs ("Bundesministerium für Arbeit und Soziales – BMAS"), 2012 (http://www.bmas.de).

2 Hans Böckler Foundation, Statistisches Taschenbuch Tarifpolitik 2012, February 2012 (http://www.boeckler.de/pdf/p_ta_tariftaschenbuch_2012.pdf).

3 Hans Böckler Foundation, Statistisches Taschenbuch Tarifpolitik 2012, February 2012 (http://www.boeckler.de/pdf/p_ta_tariftaschenbuch_2012.pdf).

Answer

The contractual partners may be 2
- associations of employers or individual employers and
- trade unions.

Question 37

Does the employer have to make the entire company aware of the collective bargaining agreement?

Answer

Yes, the employer is required to make the collective bargaining agreement public 3
that regulates the given operation in appropriate places on company grounds.

Question 38

Does the collective bargaining agreement have to be in written form?

Answer

Yes, German law requires that the collective bargaining agreement is **in written** 4
form.

Question 39

Who is legally bound by the collective bargaining agreement?

Answer

The individual employer or its employers' association and the union, as well as em- 5
ployees belonging to the given union are legally bound.

Question 40

What has to be in a collective bargaining agreement under German law?

Answer

The collective bargaining agreement contains those German legal standards that 6
can regulate the content, the conclusion and the termination of employment relationships, as well as **day-to-day company issues** and those found in and covered by the Works Constitution Act. Even the rights and obligations of the contractual partners are specified in the collective bargaining agreement.

Question 41
What rules can be set forth in a collective bargaining agreement?

Answer
7 Set forth in collective bargaining agreements are the regular, substantive **working conditions**, such as employee wages and working times, questions regarding vacation (duration of vacation time, vacation pay), the probationary period, right to bonuses, etc. It is also possible to include those rules regarding works council structure or a socially balanced layoff plan.

Question 42
When does a collective bargaining agreement apply to an individual employment relationship?

Answer
8 The collective bargaining agreement applies if, for example, both sides are bound to the collective agreement, meaning employees who are members of the union representing the given company that concluded the collective bargaining agreement and the employer who is bound to the collective bargaining agreement by its own resolution or membership in an employers' association. The collective bargaining agreement further applies, because the individual employee has agreed to a **reference in the collective bargaining agreement** in its employment contract, meaning that a particular collective bargaining agreement should find application whether the two parties are bound by the collective bargaining agreement or not (the so-called reference provision – "Bezugnahmeklausel"). A collective bargaining agreement is then also applicable if the Federal Minister for Labor and Social Affairs declares it to be generally binding.

Question 43
Can an individual employment contract deviate from the stipulations set forth by a collective bargaining agreement?

Answer
9 No, the direct and compulsory effect of the collective bargaining agreement makes deviating from it impossible. An exception could be if the deviation from the given collective bargaining agreement is to the **benefit of the employee.** A deviation from the collective bargaining agreement that is not to the benefit of the employee is only possible if that agreement finds application due to a reference provision ("Bezugnahmeklausel") and the employee consents to a change in the contract.

Question 44

Is there a registry of all German collective bargaining agreements?

Answer

Yes, and the list is kept by the German Federal Ministry of Labor and Social Affairs. 10
The conclusion, changes and nullification of the collective bargaining agreement have to be in the registry, as well as the start and end of the period the agreement being generally binding.

Question 45

What is an "opening clause" of a collective bargaining agreement? And in cases of pay and other working conditions?

Answer

The "opening clause" is a provision in a collective bargaining agreement that allows 11
for stipulations to deviate from the agreement. The stipulations that deviate from the given collective bargaining agreement can be in another collective bargaining agreement or in individual contracts.

Question 46

What are the consequences of a collective bargaining agreement not having an "opening clause"?

Answer

Alongside the German legal principle allowing for deviations from collective agree- 12
ments, **only by way of the opening clause** can the parties – employer and works council – deviate from the conditions set out in the collective bargaining agreement. Otherwise is the regulation invalid.

Chapter 5 Conclusion of an Employment Contract | Vertragsabschluss

! **Definition, Legal Principles**

As in most countries, an employment relationship in Germany is established with an employment contract. No employment contract law exists under German law. It is more the case that an employment contract is treated as a **reciprocal relationship**, as a subset of a service agreement under the German Civil Code. The employee obligates him/herself to performance and the employer to payment of a wage that has been agreed upon. Basically, an employment contract is based on the principle of freedom of contract. According to it, the parties can **freely negotiate** the content, signing and type of employment relationship. The limits of freedom of contract in Germany may be found in the principle of worker protection regulations, collective bargaining agreements, works agreements and case law.

Question 47

Do contracts need to be concluded in writing?

Answer

1 No, a **contract of employment of indefinite duration** can be concluded orally and impliedly insofar as the law, collective bargaining agreement and works agreement do not stipulate otherwise. However, the employee has the right to have basic integral parts of the contract set in writing. These **basic integral parts** of the contract are:

- name and address of the contracting parties,
- start of the employment relationship,
- place of work,
- information about the work to be performed,
- compensation,
- notification periods and applicable collective bargaining agreements when appropriate.

2 Regarding a fixed term employment contract, the limited duration has to be in written form to be valid.

Question 48

What applies if the prescribed written format is missing?

Answer

3 Employment contracts missing the prescribed form are **valid** and can be modified at any time with the consequence that subsequent agreements are legally valid, be they explicit or implicit.

4 Contrarily, agreements regarding **collective bargaining agreements** and **works agreements** are null and void if not in writing.

The missing prescribed form leads to an unfixed term employment for fixed-term contracts. 5

Question 49

Can the contract also be drafted in a language other than German?

Answer

Yes, there is no legal obligation in Germany to draft or conclude an employment contract in the German language. Despite this fact, the **language of the courts** and relevant agencies in Germany is German, so the contract would have to be translated. Nowadays, more and more contracts are **bilingually** drafted. Should that be done one of those languages should be German, as that language is the chief one in Germany. 6

Question 50

Does the employer have to draft the employment contract in the language of the foreign employee?

Answer

No, the translation of the contract into the language of a foreign employee is not required. On the other hand, the employment contract should be drafted in such a fashion that the employee can **understand the basic integral parts** of the contract. For the legal validity of the employment contract it suffices for the employee to have knowledge that the contract presented to him/her is their employment contract. If the employee has knowledge of this, the employer has fulfilled his duty to explain and consequently does not have to translate the contract or parts of it. In practice it is nevertheless commonplace in Germany to have the contract provided for **in German and English** in case of non-foreign workers. 7

Question 51

Can an employment contract be signed by the parent or holding company?

Answer

The employment contract has to be signed by the contracting parties. Employment relationships do not exist with the corporation but instead with the **individual company where the employee actually works**. A holding company can only sign an employment contract as representative, but not as the primary employer. If the employer is not a subsidiary but instead the actual parent company, then the parent company should sign the contract. 8

Question 52
Is there a minimum standard for contractual work conditions?

Answer
9 Yes, there is a law in Germany that lays out provisions to address such concerns, the so-called Act on Notification of Conditions Concerning the Employment Relationship ("Nachweisgesetz – NachwG"). Setting the fundamental contractual conditions in writing prevents ambiguities about the employment relationship and **serves as evidence** for the contracting partners in legal disputes. It represents a **duty for the employer** but not the validity of an employment contract that is only orally agreed upon.

Question 53
Can there be fixed-term employment contracts in Germany?

Answer
10 Yes, and the German Act on Part-Time Work and Fixed-Term Employment sets the conditions.[1]

Question 54
What are the conditions of a limited-term contract?

Answer
11 The limited term of an employment relationship has to be justified by a **factual reason** provided there is no exception to the two-year term limitation. There is a factual reason in the following situations:
- the company needs are only temporary;
- the short-term is only due to the employee's training or schooling;
- the given position only exists because another employee is on leave;
- the particular nature of the job to be performed calls for it being temporary;
- the limited term serves as a test;
- the person of the employee can justify the limited term;
- the employee will be compensated by budgetary resources dedicated for the given job;
- cases of new companies or with new employees who have reached their 52nd birthday by the time they commence work.

1 See also Chapter 9.

Question 55
Does the fixed term limitation have to be in writing?

Answer
The limited term of an employment contract needs to be in written form. An agreement about limiting the term that is not in writing represents a contract of employment that is of **indefinite duration.** 12

Question 56
Are there special rules for start-up companies?

Answer
Newly founded companies can limit the employment contracts to which they agree to **four years** during their first four years of existence. The **privilege** can continue to have effect through to the end of the company's eighth year. 13

Question 57
Can minors conclude a contract?

Answer
No, **consent of a legal representative** is required for the agreement's validity. Stipulations set out in the German Youth Employment Protection Act must be adhered to. So, for example, a **child under age 15** represented by his/her legal guardian cannot conclude an employment contract. However, there are exceptions for internships and vacation jobs. 14

Question 58
Does the works council need to take part in the concluding of contracts?

Answer
No, the works council has to be involved **solely** before the hiring. 15

Question 59
Does the employer have a duty to disclose information?

Answer
This duty to explain or disclose information results from the **relationship of reciprocal care** between the employer and employee. The employer's duty in respect of 16

care and supervision comes from a superior expertise or specialist's knowledge. In this respect, for example, the areas of company pension plans count here as long as it is based on an employer initiative. There will also be areas understood in this regard that are to be allocated to the employer's sphere (or responsibility), such as health risks and the avoidance of them. The employer has a **duty to inform** and explain the scope of the work to be performed and potential dangers at the workplace.

Question 60

By what standard do employment contract clauses need to be measured?

Answer

17 Employment contract clauses have to be measured by legal standards. Clauses that represent a side agreement are **subject to a content check**. These clauses cannot be made in a fashion that works against the principles of good faith and thereby unreasonably disadvantage the employee. That is the case if the employee's rights become considerably restricted by such causes. Clauses that the employee would not normally have to expect are invalid. The German General Equal Treatment Act ("Allgemeines Gleichbehandlungsgesetz – AGG") **prohibits discrimination based on race, ethnicity, gender, religion or (secular) belief, disability or sexual identity** and is thus also prohibited. Discriminatory practices are only permissible if it is vital requirement linked to the nature of the work. For example, it is permissible to limit midwife positions to females.

Question 61

What data protection regulations need to be observed?

Answer

18 Regarding the employer's right to have the most comprehensive information possible about his/her employees, the employee has a right of self-determination regarding personal data. The usage of personal data is only permissible if it is **legally provided** or takes place with the consent of the affected person. **Collection of personal data** is only allowed in an employment relationship if it is required for establishing, carrying out or ending an employment relationship. Prior consent is required, for example, in the context of an integration management program.[2]

---

2 See also Chapter 17.

Question 62
Can the content of a contract be governed by foreign law?

Answer
Yes, but the choice of legal system may not lead to the employee taking the compulsory protective measures of the country in which he/she works. The conclusion of an employment contract that accords with foreign law cannot, for example, work around German regulations regarding protections of unfair dismissal, maternity or of the severely handicapped.[3] 19

Question 63
When can an employment contract be contested?

Answer
An employment contract can be contested with the **presentation of errors** in content, declaration of intent or when there are **mistakes about the characteristics of the document**, or in cases of **fraudulent misrepresentation.** Contesting an employment contract due to fraudulent misrepresentation implies that the party accused of avoidance has lied about a matter of fact in an impermissible manner. If the employer asks the employee an impermissible question (i.e. regarding pregnancy) that employer is not entitled to appeal.[4] 20

Question 64
When is an employment contract void?

Answer
An employment contract is void when there is a violation of the law or bona mores, lacking legal capacity to contract or after an appeal. 21

Question 65
What does a foreign employee have to do prior to arrival in Germany in order from him/her to work under a German contract? Does a foreign employee require a special work permit if he/she wishes to work in Germany?

---

3 See also Part 1 margin number 26.
4 See also Chapter 3.

Answer

22 The rule allowing the free movement of workers for **workers from EU states** makes a **work permit unnecessary**. Workers from Romania, Croatia or Bulgaria have to apply for a residency permit that allows for employment for the period they want to work. Generally speaking, workers that are **citizens of non-EU or EEA have to apply for a registered stay permit** at the German Aliens Registration Office.[5] The access to the German job market for these foreign workers is determined by the German Residency Act regulations as well as approved Employment Regulations and Employment Procedure Regulations.

23 Therefore, only non-EU or EEA citizens need to take extra steps in order to work under a German contract.[6]

5 See also Chapter 29.

6 See also Chapter 29.

Chapter 6 Disciplinary Warning | Abmahnung

Definition, Legal Principles

A disciplinary warning is a **management tool**. Legally, it is the precursor to a behavior-based regular dismissal or an extraordinary for cause. A disciplinary warning exists, then, if an employer points out a poor performance of work to an employee in a **clear and recognizable manner**. And, such a warning has to be given at a time which chronologically corresponds with the breach of contractual duties.

Through the disciplinary warning, the employee should be reminded of his/her contractual duties and warned about the consequences of further violations. For evidentiary purposes, the disciplinary warning should always be **made in writing**. If the employee is not in agreement with the disciplinary warning, he/she may go before a labor court to have the disciplinary warning removed from his/her personnel file.

Question 66

What is a disciplinary warning understood to be in Germany?

Answer

A disciplinary warning is **not regulated by law**. It is understood as an employer's formal request to the employee to refrain from or perform a concretely denoted act when legal consequences are threatened. As in many other countries, it has the **function of warning** the employee. 1

Question 67

What cannot be classified as a disciplinary warning?

Answer

No disciplinary warnings are 2
- co-worker suggestions;
- instructions;
- remonstrances;
- admonishments and
- reprimands.

Question 68

Does an employer have to give disciplinary warnings?

Answer

The employer is only obligated to give disciplinary warnings if the employee has 3
culpably carried out an infringement of contractual duties and for that reason the

employer contemplates dismissal for reasons of conduct. The disciplinary warning and the repetition of the bad behavior is a **prerequisite for the validity of dismissal** as it supports to reason the perceived breach of contract.

Question 69
How often can disciplinary warnings be issued?

Answer
4 Theoretically, the employer can issue a disciplinary warning for each instance of acting contrary to contract. Multiple written disciplinary warnings due to breaches of responsibility of the same kind for which no consequences result serve to **weaken the effect of the warning** so that termination of the employee is no longer possible despite further contractual violations. The employer should therefore assess how often he/she wishes to give disciplinary warnings prior to providing notice of dismissal.

Question 70
Does a disciplinary warning have to be in written form?

Answer
5 No, a disciplinary warning may come in different forms. It can also come verbally. An exception exists when, for example, a collective agreement provides otherwise. For **evidentiary purposes**, the disciplinary warning must be given in writing. The description of the letter as disciplinary warning is not required. That said, a specific description is advisable for purposes of clarity.

Question 71
What needs to be stated in the disciplinary warning?

Answer
6 The disciplinary warning has to **concretely state the misconduct**. General accusations are insufficient. Future behavior in accordance with the contract has to be formulated. The consequences in case of recurrence are also to be outlined. It suffices if it is made unmistakably clear that the employment relationship is endangered in case of a reoccurrence of the given violating act.

Question 72
Who may issue a disciplinary warning?

Answer

The individual with the right to issue a disciplinary warning is someone who is authorized to discipline the affected person. Beyond the **manager**, immediate **supervisors** may be that person. The **legal counsel** authorized for this purpose is also entitled. 7

Question 73

Who may not receive a disciplinary warning?

Answer

The **individual tasked with data protection** may not receive a disciplinary warning addressing his/her data protection duties. A **member of the works council** may not receive a disciplinary warning if the accusation of his acting contrary to contract relates to his work as a works council member. 8

Question 74

What rights does the warned employee have?

Answer

That employee can have a **counter-reply** placed into his personnel file. Further, the employee can **request the deletion or withdrawal** of the disciplinary warning and have such action judicially enforced if the given warning is unjustified. The employee can immediately retract a disciplinary warning if it contains defamatory statements. 9

Question 75

When is a disciplinary warning unjustified?

Answer

This is the case if one or more of the following applies: 10

- the disciplinary warning is not made in proper fashion that accords with regulations;
- it contains untrue statements of fact;
- it is based on erroneous assessment of employee behavior;
- the German principle of proportionality has been harmed, which, under German Employment Law, would mean that
  - the employee has failed to make clear the rational relation between his/her means and the objective for the warning;
  - the employer chose means that failed to keep the impairment of employee rights to a minimum;

  - what is achieved was not proportional to the price with respect to infringement of rights;
- lastly, no defensible interest of the employer exists or the disciplinary warning contains generalized accusations.

Question 76
What happens to the employer if a disciplinary warning is proven to be unjustified?

Answer
11 The disciplinary warning is to be **removed from the personnel file**. It cannot be used for notice of termination for reasons of conduct. In such a case, the dismissal would be invalid.

Chapter 7 Dismissal | Arbeitgeberkündigung

Definition, Legal Principles

!

Dismissal represents a **one-sided ending** of an employment relationship. What one must differentiate is immediate dismissal, or one for extraordinary circumstances without notice ("außerordentliche Kündigung"), and ordinary ("ordentliche Kündigung") dismissal. An **ordinary dismissal** represents for both employer and employee the regular means of ending an employment relationship. On the other hand, an **immediate dismissal** is an exceptional means of ending employment relationships that have become unreasonable in nature and are for a discernibly important reason and, as a rule, is performed without notice. An immediate dismissal is uniformly regulated in sec. 626 of the German Civil Code for all types of employment relationships and is guaranteed as a **constitutionally protected right** to freedom for both contracting partners. An ordinary dismissal that takes place within a set time period generally does not require grounds for the dismissal. That only applies, however, beyond the scope of the German Employment Protection Act ("Kündigungsschutzgesetz"). So long as the law finds application, reasons that rule out an unfair dismissal must exist. Then, the dismissal can only take place for operational reasons or on grounds of personal capability. The exact criteria for socially unjustified dismissals is defined by the German Labor Court.

According to sec. 623 of the German Civil Code, all dismissals must be **in writing**.

I. General Aspects

Question 77

Upon whom do the norms set out in the German Unfair Dismissal Act find application?

Answer

The German Unfair Dismissal Act finds application on those who work for operations that regularly have **more than ten employees** who are working for more than six months annually. For operations that have more than five employees, the German Unfair Dismissal Act finds unlimited application only for those employees who began their employment relationship before January 1, 2004. 1

Question 78

What notice periods apply under German law?

Answer

Notice periods in Germany are not uniformly regulated. They are found for example in the German Civil Code, special legal provisions, collective bargaining agreements, and in employment contracts. The **statutory minimum notice period** for employees who have completed their probationary period is **four weeks.** If the employer terminates the employee, the notice period depends on the length of the em- 2 ployment relationship and is **between one and seven months**. For the severely handicapped a notice period of four weeks is to be kept in mind. A collective bargaining agreement can lead to a variation in these notice periods.

Question 79
What notice period applies for a probationary period?

Answer
3 German law prescribes a period of **two weeks** as a rule. Collective bargaining agreements often contain longer periods.

Question 80
Can resignation from or termination of employment take place before the employment relationship begins?

Answer
4 Yes, the employee's resignation from a job or an employer terminating someone is possible before the employment relationship actually begins. According to German Federal Labor Court **case law**, the beginning of the notice period in which an employer must comply is based on the **will of the parties**. If there are shorter periods in the employment contract, the **beginning of the notice period** is presumed to begin upon receipt of notice and not when work actually commenced.

Question 81
When does the employee have to receive notice?

Answer
5 Immediate dismissal for cause or extraordinary dismissal has to take place within two weeks after the party entitled to dismiss has acquired knowledge of the material facts for the dismissal. For an ordinary dismissal, such as one for poor performance, there is **no statutorily defined deadline**. The employer's **right of termination is forfeited**, however, if he/she delays on taking action for a longer time and thereby arouses legitimate confidence in the employee that the dismissal is not going to happen.

Question 82
Can a short-term employment contract be canceled?

Answer

Based on legal principles, a short-term employment contract cannot be terminated. There would need to be a clear statement in either an individual or collective bargaining agreement for that to happen. 6

Question 83

Does termination have to be in writing? Is an e-mail or fax sufficient?

Answer

Yes, the termination of employment has to be **in writing signed by hand** or by way of a **notarially certified mark.** A signed e-mail or fax does not suffice. 7

Question 84

Who has to sign the termination letter?

Answer

The termination letter has to be **hand-signed by the employer.** As a rule, this is the company's principal or its board of directors. Note: the principal (e.g. GM/CEO) may send an **authorized representative** but he/she should present a letter of authorization to dismiss employees. This is not required if the principal has informed the employee about the power of attorney being granted to a proxy, or the employee already has knowledge about the proxy. For this requirement it suffices if the proxy named in the commercial register signs in the manner prescribed there. 8

Question 85

Where does the employee need to receive the notice?

Answer

The notice of termination can be given to the employee or an authorized third party, be it at the workplace or mailed via postal service to the employee's residence. Delivery is considered to have taken place if the termination notice reaches **a place where the recipient can reasonably anticipate it.** In cases where it has been given to a third party or put into a mailbox, the notice of termination is considered delivered at the point when acknowledgement can be expected, e.g. the emptying of the mailbox. 9

Question 86

When can employees not be terminated by notice?

Answer

10 Employees are not terminable by ordinary notice when they **cannot be dismissed using the same protocol** that would be used for most employees. For example, works council members, youth and trainee representatives and severely handicapped may not be terminated by ordinary notice. Non-terminability can even be agreed upon in collective bargaining or individual agreements, by, for example, linking it to employment with the company.

11 The inability of being able to be terminated by notice **does not preclude immediate dismissal for cause.** In individual cases, then, the ordinary termination process finds application in cases of immediate dismissal for cause.

Question 87

Can the employer who is on vacation at the time be terminated?

Answer

12 Yes, absence due to the employee being on vacation **does not preclude a notice of termination.** Neither does it prevent the receipt of the notice of termination in the employee's absence.

Question 88

Can the termination of employment be revoked by an employer?

Answer

13 No, as a unilateral declaration of intent that has to be received cannot revoke the legal force of received termination letter. The revocation of termination is to be seen as **a request for a new employment relationship**.

II. Extraordinary and Ordinary Dismissal

Question 89

What types of notice are there?

Answer

14 A distinction is made between ordinary dismissal ("ordentliche Kündigung") and immediate dismissal for cause ("außerordentliche Kündigung").

Question 90

What is an "außerordentliche Kündigung"?

Answer

Described in English, an "außerordentliche Kündigung" is a dismissal that termi- 15
nates the contractual relationship **for good cause** without observing a notice period. Sometimes referred to in English as an extraordinary dismissal, it may only take place when taking into account both factors relevant to the circumstances of the particular case and the **interests of both parties**, and that the terminating party cannot be reasonably expected to continue working until the notice period expires or the agreed expiration of the contract.

Question 91

Is there a time limit to keep for extraordinary dismissals?

Answer

Normally, a two-week notice period is the time limit applied, which means that the 16
person giving notice only has **two weeks after having securing knowledge** of the facts that leads to the dismissal to declare the employment relationship terminated. Individual legal regulations and collective bargaining agreements can reduce this notice period even further.

Question 92

What are the reasons for ordinary dismissal?

Answer

The German Unfair Dismissal Act ("Kündigungsschutzgesetz") provides **three rea-** 17
sons for a socially justified dismissal, the standard that must be met for an ordinary dismissal:

- operational reasons,
- behavioral reasons, or
- those based on the person of the employee (i.e. the employee is unable to do the job).

Should the German Unfair Dismissal Act not apply, the dismissal has to be judged 18
solely in accordance with the German principles of good faith ("Treu und Glauben") and good morals ("gute Sitten").

Question 93

Do the reasons for dismissal need to be in the written notice?

Answer

19 Generally speaking, the reasons for the dismissal are not in a **termination letter**. As a result the employee sometimes does not know why he was dismissed. An exception would be cases of extraordinary dismissals, in which instance the **employee can request a statement of reasons** for termination; the missing information does not influence the validity of the dismissal but could lead to **employee damage claims.** It is indeed very rare that this might lead to compensation for damages. It could happen, however, in cases where the employee files a suit against the dismissal, loses the case and later claims that he/she would have not filed a claim if he/she had known the reasons.

III. Protection against Dismissal

Question 94

What general protections of employees against dismissal exist in Germany?

Answer

20 For starters, the legislature only considers certain reasons of termination permissible. Employers have special requirements to observe depending on the grounds for termination. In cases of dismissal for operational reasons, the employer has a **social selection procedure** to carry out, and **must explain** the business decisions that lead to the elimination of positions. A **warning** is required as part of a termination for behavioral reasons. In cases of termination for reasons related to the person of the employee, the employer has to do everything within his/her power to avoid terminating the given employment relationship.

Question 95

What special protections of employees against dismissal exist in Germany?

Answer

21 Special protections against dismissal appear in the **protections of certain groups of people.** These groups enjoy protection from ordinary.[1]

Question 96

What applies for pregnant women?

---

1 See also Question 86 – When can employees not be terminated by notice?, margin number 10.

Answer

The agreement of the body authorized according to state law ("Landesrecht") has **to be asked for approval** before dismissing a pregnant employee. This depends on the state or regional governments or regional council. A dismissal carried out without the necessary approval is invalid and cannot be remedied. 22

Question 97

Can a severely handicapped employee be terminated?

Answer

Yes, a severely handicapped person's employment relationship can be terminated. 23
That said, severely handicapped persons working in Germany enjoy a special protection against unfair dismissal. This stipulates **special requirements regarding the type of dismissal**, such as obtaining the approval of the German Integration Offices ("Integrationsamt") for the dismissal. One carried out without the necessary approval is invalid and cannot be remedied.

Question 98

Can a works council member have his/her employment terminated?

Answer

Works Council members enjoy a **special protection from unfair dismissal**. The ordi- 24
nary dismissal of a works council member is not possible. Indeed works council members can only be **terminated by extraordinary means**, which means that the employer has to demonstrate that continuing the employment relationship is unreasonable.

Question 99

Can the employer fire an employee because he/she is unable to work due to illness?

Answer

Yes, dismissal due to an illness preventing the ability to work represents a dismissal for 25
reasons related to the person of the employee. It only comes into question if the **illness seriously impacts the employment relationship**. This may be the case if the performance of work is not possible for a longer time (1.5 years) or if the duration of the inability to work due to illness is principally short but recurrent. Plainly stated, the employer is not be expected to wait indefinitely for the recovery of the employee (**principle of proportionality**). What is decisive here is the requirement of having a clearly negative prognosis for the development of the employee according to objective standards. The point in time of the dismissal is decisive for the prognosis.

Question 100
Can an older employee be dismissed because he/she works more slowly than his/her co-workers?

Answer
26 Firing a so-called "low performer" is only possible under the **strictest conditions.** The most important point here is what work the employer can fairly expect. With older employees it is common that their work performance diminishes. Dismissal of the employee for such reasons would be seen as being in violation of the principles of social considerations stipulated by German labor law.

IV. Obligations of the Employer in case of Dismissal

Question 101
Does the employer have to provide a letter of reference?

Answer
27 Yes, the employer is obligated to provide a reference letter.

Question 102
Which documents does the employer have to provide in case of dismissal?

Answer
28 The employer has to provide an **interim reference letter** for the application process, as well as a **final reference letter** on the employee's work. Due to a secondary obligation derived from German Employment Law, the employer must also provide a **statement of income.**

29 The employer has to demonstrate all of the facts that could be considered with respect to the decision about a claim to **unemployment pay or a transitional allowance** by the time employment has been concluded. Further, the employer has to provide the employee with a report of the given calendar year's **used and remaining vacation time.**

Question 103
Does the employer have to give the employee a disciplinary warning before giving notice of dismissal?

Answer

An advanced disciplinary warning is required in scope of **dismissal for behavior** in ordinary conditions. The requirement of a disciplinary warning results from the prevailing principle of proportionality found in the German Unfair Dismissal Act. A dismissal should be the last resort (principle of ultima ratio). The **employer has to inform the employee** of his/her wrongdoing ("Rüge", or written reprimand) and through this afford him/her the chance to act in a manner conforming to the contract in the future ("Ermahnung", or verbal caution). Secondly, the employer has to **make the employee aware that his/her job is in danger** if he repeats the given behavior ("Warnung", or warning). There is no obligation to warn if the employer cannot achieve his/her intended aims with warnings (i.e. written reprimand, verbal caution, warning). 30

V. Involvement of the Works Council and the Boards of Directors

Question 104

Does the works council or union have to be heard regarding a dismissal?

Answer

If the company has a works council, the given works council has to be informed **before the notification of dismissal** is made. Union input is not required for a dismissal. 31

Question 105

Can the employer dismiss an employee if the works council objects?

Answer

It is true that the objection of the works council does not prevent an employer from dismissing an employee. However, a works council objection for an ordinary dismissal provides the **right to continued employment** with the employer until a legally binding conclusion of the legal dispute. 32

Question 106

What applies to dismissal during the probationary period?

Answer

The company also has to **inform the works council** before notifying an employee of termination during the probationary period. 33

Question 107
Does the board of directors have to be heard regarding a dismissal?

Answer
34 The board of directors does **not have to be heard** regarding a dismissal. Occasional personnel measures by executives can require the approval of the board of directors.

VI. En Masse Layoffs

Question 108
What does the employee need to keep in mind if a large number of employees are going to be laid off (en masse layoffs, or "Massenentlassung")?

Answer
35 In cases of en masse layoffs, the employer has an obligation to notify of and receive consultation on the decision. The employer has to **report the en masse layoff to the German Federal Employment Agency** and the works council and share with the works council information about the **layoff plans**. In Germany, a mass layoff is considered en masse if an employer with 21 to 59 employees wishes to lay off five of them, with 60 to 499 wishes to lay off 10%, or one with at least 500 employees wishes to lay off at least 30 employees.

Question 109
If an employer is laying people off, does that employer have to release employees from having to work in order to search for a job?

Answer
36 There is an obligation under German law to release employees to search for another job if the release from having to work takes place in what the employer considers a reasonable scope with an ongoing payment obligation. However, employees have the **right to continue their work** until termination date. The employer cannot release them from their duty of works without valid reasons.

VII. Legal Action against Dismissal

Question 110
What happens if the employee files a complaint regarding his/her dismissal?

Answer

Legal action for dismissal allows the person dismissed the **possibility of invalidating the dismissal**. If the person dismissed does not assert a claim before the German Labor Court **within three weeks** after having received the termination letter that the employment relationship has not been terminated by the given notice of termination, the notice of termination is considered legally effective from the outset. 37

Question 111

Can documents that are not in German language be provided to the German courts?

Answer

No, the judicial language is German. Submitting documents that are not in German is legally insufficient. They have to be **translated**. 38

Chapter 8 Employee Liability | Arbeitnehmerhaftung

Definition, Legal Principles
Employee liability deals with whether or if, then in what scope, the employee can be made responsible for damages that occurred in the course of carrying out his/her work. If the work-related accident involves damage to persons, the right to statutory accident insurance comes into play (German Social Security Code – "SGB VII"). For all other damages the authority of principles developed by **case law** on internal compensatory damages apply.

Question 112
What is meant with employee liability in Germany?

Answer
1 The term employee liability deals with the scope and under what conditions the employee has to compensate the employer for damages the employee caused in the process of carrying out his/her work in a **non-compliant fashion**.

Question 113
For what is the employee liable to the employer?

Answer
2 The scope of the liability is based on the **degree of the blame**. In cases of minor negligence – thus, less attributable blame – the employee is not liable, e.g. in cases of typical going astray ("typisches Abirren"), offending someone else ("sich vergreifen"), misspeaking ("sich versprechen") or making a mistake ("sich vertun").[1] In cases of moderate negligence – thus, moderate attributable blame – the employee has **proportionate liability**. In order to calculate the loss ratio, the totality of the circumstances of the given situation (amount of damages, predisposition to/risk of danger, etc.) has to be factored in (e.g. with damages to a company vehicle, it is of significance whether the employer has full comprehensive insurance. He/she is not obligated, therefore the non-conclusion of analysis at the expense of the employer in the given situation can be of considerable importance; the employee is only liable for the deductible, which would have been negotiable upon signing a comprehensive insurance agreement). In gross negligence cases, employee liability is unlimited unless he/she is deemed worthy of (legal) protection ("schutzwürdig"), e.g. forgetting an unsecured briefcase at a restaurant, driving under the influence of

1 German Federal Labor Court ("Bundesarbeitsgericht – BAG"), ruling dated October 28, 2010 – 8 AZR 418/09 –.

alcohol, driving through a red light. If the employee handled in accordance with rules and regulations, he has **unlimited liability**.

Question 114
How is the risk of liability shared between employer and employee?

Answer
Risk of liability is shared between employer and employee. A proportion is normally 3
determined by **mutual agreement** of the employer and employee; courts decide in cases of dispute. How high the employee's portion is depends on the circumstances of the particular situation. That means that German law gives consideration of circumstances that work in favor of and against the employee, e.g. past actions, type and difficulty of the task, level of damage, risk of damage.

Question 115
Can there be a limit to liability for the employee?

Answer
Only **in exceptional cases** can there be a limit to liability. It is the case if the em- 4
ployee's earnings are in clear disproportion to the liability risk of the task. Only in exceptional cases can there be a limit to liability. It is the case if the employee's earnings are in clear disproportion to the liability risk of the task. The limitation of liability with gross negligence will not be precluded by the German Federal Labor Court in these cases. Whether and to what extent the loss ratio appears justified, is to be judged in respect to the violation of obligation and the amount of damages. The German Federal Labor Court has not imposed a loss ratio that exceeds the **annual income** of the affected person. For example: four months salary in an automobile accident, twelve months salary for a minijob.

Chapter 9 Fixed-term | Befristung

Definition, Legal Principles[1]

The trend towards more flexible forms of work is reflected in the increasing number of fixed-term employment relationships. In Germany, **permissibility of a time limit** is comprehensively regulated by the Part-time Work and Fixed-term Employment Contracts Act ("Teilzeit- und Befristungsgesetz").

Negotiations on fixed-term employment must be in writing. An employment relationship can be limited either by the calendar or an objective reason. A term limit without explicitly stated reasons may not exceed **three extensions within a two-year period**. Further, limiting the term of employment is always permissible if the material grounds provided are justified.

Question 116

What are the conditions of a limited-term contract?

Answer

1 The limited term of an employment relationship has to be **justified by a factual reason** provided there is no exception to the two-year term limitation. There is a factual reason in the following situations:

- company needs are only temporary;
- the short-term is only due to the employee's training or schooling;
- the given position only exists because another employee is on leave;
- the particular nature of the job to be performed calls for it being temporary;
- the limited term serves as a test;
- the person of the employee can justify the limited term (i.e. the employee has limited abilities geared for the given tasks at hand);
- the employee will be compensated by the set budgetary resources dedicated for the given job;
- cases of new companies or with new employees who have reached their 52nd birthday by the time they commence work.

Question 117

Does the fixed term limitation have to be in writing?

Answer

2 The limited term of an employment contract needs to be in written form. An agreement about limiting the term that is not in writing represents a contract of employment that is of **indefinite duration**.

---

1 For further information about the retirement plan, see Chapter 28.

Chapter 10 Freelancer | Freie Mitarbeiter

Definition, Legal Principles

Self-employed persons, or freelancers, form a third pillar to the German employment structure next to the classic employment of workers in the private and public sectors. As the number of typical employment relationships decrease, the number of jobs that are **atypical forms of employment**, such as freelancing, is steadily increasing. Indeed, freelancers are being used in **diverse business sectors**. For example, there are more than 70,000 freelancers working in the IT sector, but they are also becoming more commonly used in areas like the music, advertising, event planning/management or the cosmetic and pharmaceutical industries.

The English term "freelancer" has become **common in everyday German**, though the German terms "freie Mitarbeiter" or "Selbstständige" are also used. The common understanding of a freelancer describes a person who carries out jobs for a company **without being an employee** of that company.

Question 118

What are typical characteristics of a freelancer?

Answer

A freelancer carries out his/her business as work for him/herself and in his/her own name. With this arrangement, there is **no employer-employee relationship** between the freelancer and the client taking on the freelancer. There is, however, **no legal definition** for the term freelancer. German case law nevertheless developed **certain criteria** as part of a differentiating freelancers from employees that define the work of a freelancer as being opposite. 1

Question 119

What exactly is the difference between a freelancer and an employee under German law?

Answer

In the following breakdown, German case law provides more evidence of **what an employment relationship is** than that of a freelancer: 2

- the client establishes the precise purpose of content and scope of work to be performed;
- strict timeline from the client, such as those which may come in the form of service plans that will not cause participation by employees;
- the client's authority to give instructions regarding location from which work is to be performed;
- the assumption of no economic risks whatsoever by the employees;

- the requirements to coordinate any vacation time approved by the client;
- agreement on a ban on secondary employment.

3 However, it comes down to the **circumstances of the particular situation**. If the aforementioned proof is available, it does **not necessarily** mean that an employment relationship and not a freelancer agreement exists.

Question 120
What's the difference between a freelancer and a so-called "Freiberufler"?

Answer
4 Under German law, there are **two sorts** of what English speakers would term "freelancers". The first type of freelancer ("Selbstständige") only refers to the **type of employment**, while the other type of freelancer ("Freiberufler") relates to the **type of work performed**, that is, the practice of a particular profession. Some professions which count as "Freiberufe" include physicians, attorneys or tax advisers. A list of the "freie Berufe" can be found in sec. 18 of the German Tax Code.

Question 121
Are freelancers in Germany entitled to continued remuneration when out ill?

Answer
5 In Germany only employees are entitled to continued remuneration when out ill. For the most part, a freelancer is only remunerated **for the work he/she actually does.** It is nevertheless possible that a freelancer and his/her client arrive at an agreement on sick pay in a contract.

Question 122
Do the regulations regarding a works agreement or collective bargaining rights apply at all to freelancers?

Answer
6 Since the freelancer is not an employee, the regulations regarding a works agreement or collective bargaining rights **generally do not apply** to freelancers.

7 Independent of this, clients (employers) still have the **obligation to inform** the works council. He/she is therefore obligated to inform the works council if a freelancer contract is to be extended for work at the given company. The works council can then check if any **oversight or co-determination rights** exist with respect to the usage of the freelancer.

Question 123
What advantages does the employer have if using a freelancer?

Answer
Freelancers principally take into account the **organizational flexibility** that an increasing number of workers seek, whose abilities are temporarily called upon and which can be further optimized due to changes in demands for specialization in company production processes. 8

The advantages for the client include: 9
- not having a permanent employment contract commitment;
- employment protection regulations are not applicable;
- no non-wage labor costs;
- personnel planning reliability;
- targeted expertise usage;
- depending on the basis of contract, right for warranties and to claim against defects for bad work;
- the possibility of a targeted calculation of costs.

Question 124
How can a contract with a freelancer be structured?

Answer
Freelancers can be put to work for the client on the basis of a **local or service contract**. Remuneration can be made according to a fixed-price contract, flat-rate payment arrangement or pay based on cost and materials used. Whichever type of contract is chosen does not matter in the end. What does matter for employment status is the **actual execution of the work**. The contract is merely a piece of evidence that there is an agreement between the two parties. Should the contents of the contract contradict the actual execution, the latter is what counts under German law. Using freelancer contract ("Freelancer-Vertrag") as heading or a describing the work to be done as freelancer work ("Freelancer-Tätigkeit") does not suffice for an incontestable classification as freelancer work. 10

Question 125
What is a "Scheinvertrag"?

Answer
A "Scheinvertrag", which can be translated to be a **fictitious or sham contract**, exists in cases when the contract is set up as a freelancer contract and its actually execution is to be made as a traditional employment contract. The same ap- 11

plies if it emerges that the contract **practically functioned as an employment contract.**

Question 126

What are the contractual don'ts for a freelancer contract?

Answer

12 Here are some of the contractual don'ts for a freelancer contract:
- setting of working times and places;
- participation in the time-keeping system;
- performing or providing of services by only a specific person;
- utilization of travel cost guidelines;
- employee-like limitations to liability;
- obligation to authorize vacation.

Question 127

How can a fictitious contract be corrected?

Answer

13 The parties can correct a fictitious contract in which they adapt it **to befit legal freelancer work** and that the contractual relationship is correspondingly carried out. Another way would be to **convert the contract into a normal employment contract** with all its rights and responsibilities.

Question 128

With which German court can a freelancer file a complaint against the client?

Answer

14 German labor courts only address complaints by employees, so freelancers have to **call upon civil courts** in disputes with their client. For pure claims for establishing an employment relationship with the client, however, the labor courts have jurisdiction. The **mere legal opinion** of the complainant, should it be the employee, does not suffice for affirming the jurisdiction of the labor courts.

Chapter 11 Home-Office | Heimarbeit

Definition, Legal Principles
Like in many other places, a home office is simply considered an office in the home. In the sense understood here, a home office is when **work due** in accordance with an employment contract is performed at home. This differs from telecommuting and working out of the home as, according to the Homeworking Act ("Heimarbeitsgesetz"), home office usage is not to be agreed as a place to perform company work at the employee's home on a permanent basis. Instead, a home office is only **chosen for one-off situations.**

In the last few years the term home office has been used increasingly more and more in German, particularly in cases where the employee has the possibility to complete his/her contractually agree upon work at home or elsewhere outside of the workplace in certain situations (e.g. when out due to sick children, work is being done on the employee's home, peaks in workload).

Question 129
What are the advantages of implementing a home office in Germany?

Answer
By way of a **flexible choice of place of work**, the employee is presented with an 1
opportunity to perhaps establish a **better work-life balance.**

From the employer's standpoint, a home office serves as a **employee retention** 2
program and causes a reduction in absences as well as an increase of employer's desirability. Home offices can also serve as a reasonable **solution to limited office space** at company work sites.

Question 130
What are the disadvantages to home offices?

Answer
Employers relinquish managerial prerogatives with respect to place where work is to be 3
performed. With this employers generally **give up the chance to check work** regarding not only place but also time performed, as well as other working conditions (e.g. keeping to company policies, confidentiality obligations and the secure maintenance of files and papers). Accordingly, making use of a home office assumes considerably more trust in the employee(s). It requires a considerable **sense of responsibility**, and consideration and demands requires from the employee and management a **painstaking weighting of company and employee interests** in every individual situation.

Question 131
Do employees in Germany have a right to a home office?

Answer

4 No, employees have **no legal right** to entitlement to a temporary home office.

Question 132

How can the chance to have a home office be agreed to as a part of the employment relationship?

Answer

5 Generally speaking, the employer can, among other things, determine the place, time, content and type of work contractually due in accordance with his/her **managerial prerogatives** ("Direktionsrecht") set forth in the German Trade Regulations Act, so long as no other contractual rights or ones granted by the German Works Constitution Act exist. As a rule employers establish one or more of his/her work sites as places of work. As stated earlier, the employer **gives up quite a bit of his/her managerial prerogatives** with respect to the place where work is to be performed with the implementation of a home office. And, the employer does not have a one-sided right to intervene in an employee's right to title or possession or in his/her private life. In accordance with this, the employer is deprived of meddling with the home of the employer. Consequently, the implementation of a home office requires the employee and employer to **mutually agree upon rules**. These can be made in different ways according to how many employees should enjoy the right to work from home, how the arrangement is in detail and what binding effects are intended. One idea for these situations is a structure put into an **individual contract** with the employee, **unilateral employer guidelines** or a **works/site agreement**.

6 Independent of which form of home office the employer decides on, the arrangement of the following provisions need to be settled:

- the scope of the home office;
- the scope of what the personal sphere is;
- conditions of home office use (especially amount of prior notice employees must give employers before establishing a home office);
- home office work space and times;
- issues of confidentiality and data protection;
- and the right to withdraw from the arrangement ("Widerrufsvorbehalt").

Question 133

What individual agreement provisions or guidelines are to be kept in mind with the implementation of a home office?

Answer

The **principles** found in the Act Governing General Business Conditions ("Allgemeine Geschäftsbedingungen – AGB") are to be kept in mind if the chance of establishing a home office presents itself by way of: 7

- individual agreement provisions with the employee (e.g. in employment contract or through an additional agreement to the same effect), **or**
- through an employer guideline.

The provisions have to be formulated in a correspondingly **transparent and unambiguous** fashion and **not represent an unreasonable disadvantage** for the employee. 8

Question 134

What needs to be kept in mind with respect to the scope of a home office?

Answer

At the time a home office is implemented the scope of what work is to be performed within the established working hours are to be or may be performed in the domestic working setting needs to be set. What comes into question is the **general definition** that a home office is permitted "temporarily" or "in exceptional cases". However, if the employee (e.g. after returning from parental leave) is given the option of establishing a set days to work from a home office, a **limitation of telecommuting** is required. If a certain amount of working hours be completed in a home office, at least a partial telecommuting employment arrangement is to be approved, with the consequence that the subsequently applicable rules are to be considered. 9

In Germany, telecommuting is understood to be **every form of work that takes place away from the central work station** at the employer's work site. Telecommuting is, so far as German Employment law is concerned, of a **neutral status**. It can be done by freelancers or home office workers or with a traditional employment relationship. The "employee" is therefore engaged in telecommuting if the general conditions applied to the term employee are fulfilled; this means that he/she is not in a self-employed relationship with the employer and is subject to the employer's directives and is for these reasons personally dependent. Consequently, **employment laws are applicable** to this legal relationship. If, on the other hand, there is an absence of personal dependence, the telecommuter can, according to the Home Working Act, be considered a "home worker" if the other conditions of the Home Working Act are met. It is significant to note that there are always considerations made for **special cases**. 10

Should a specific portion of an employee's working hours be performed out of a home office, this can at least **partially substantiate a telecommuting employ-** 11

ment arrangement under the aforementioned terms with the consequence that the subsequently applicable conditions and regulations (especially the German Home Working Act) are to be borne in mind. Here, the special situation that should be kept in mind in terms of a home office is that it suffices for the incorporation of a home office employee in the operational organization – and thus the existence of an employment relationship – if the telecommuter is instructed to carry out his work for the employer with that employer's resources and works with other company employees. Later changes with regard to the scope of time for work in the domestic setting have to be **mutually set** by employer and employee. The scope of work to be performed from a home office should be **put in writing** for purposes of legal clarity and burden of proof.

Question 135

What needs to be kept in mind in terms of granting an employee permission to have a home office?

Answer

12 With the adoption of a home office the **employer has to decide** which employees can have home offices, be that all employees, specific groups of them, specific departments, or even those in their probationary period or those with limited-term contracts. In this context the employer needs to keep in mind that not all departments of a company are suited for home offices. The specific work performance of an employee or group of employees has to be **appropriate for a home office arrangement** to go into effect. The employer can, for example, plan **department-specific exceptions** or only permit home offices for certain groups, e.g. field or sales representatives.

13 What also needs to be clarified is to what extent individuals who are in vocational training part of their careers should be allowed to work from a home office without **endangering the educational value** of their traineeship.

14 The employer should further think about whether or not those who are on probation should be allowed to work from a home office. This suggests that a home office arrangement **can be tested out** with the employee from the start. An argument against such an arrangement is that the difficulties of integrating the new employee into the company will be compounded by the extensive time away from the office. Contacts to co-workers and the works council, not to mention identification with the organization in general, can be impaired. Furthermore, the **cost of establishing a home office** (e.g. making laptops available) can possibly arise, costs that would be avoided for other unsuccessful probationary periods. The same question comes to the fore with limited-term contract workers.

Question 136
What should be considered when setting the conditions of possible home office usage?

Answer
The employer should establish the general framework for the possible usage of a home office. This means that he/she has to **establish rules** on how and under which conditions the usage of a home office even comes into question. 15

16 If intended, an **approval procedure** has to be arranged. Should, for example, the prior consent of the superior(s), department head, manager, etc. be necessary? In what form should the consent be obtained? On the basis of compliance **written form** is recommended, which includes e-mail or by way of an application form.

17 Additionally, **prior notice** should be given so that the employer can prepare for the employee only being available on a limited basis. Depending on the type of business, this can be between one or multiple workdays notice. It is also worth considering what counts for **urgent or special cases**. For those cases it can be agreed that agreement by phone or subsequent approval is permissible.

18 A condition for using a home office should in each case be the **accessibility of the employee** by e-mail or telephone, so that the employer can, for example, give instructions or obtain updated information.

Question 137
What has to be kept in mind when arranging a home office working space?

Answer
19 By agreeing to allow the employer to do his/her work from a home office, a **home becomes a place of work**. With this comes a few employer and employee obligations. For starters, the German Occupational Health and Safety Act is fully applicable so long we are dealing with an employee or an employee-like individual in the sense of the German Labor Court Act (with the exception of home businesses). According to the German Occupational Health and Safety Act, the employer is obligated to, "meet the **required workplace safety measures** with consideration of the circumstances that impact the health and safety of the worker at the workplace." Also, the special obligations to cooperate apply to the employee. Practically speaking, this means that the employee has to set up an ergonomic workplace as a condition of being allowed to have a home office. In light of this it is recommended to ensure in the agreement with the employee who is to be using a home office that his/her home satisfies the pertinent legal regulations. It is the **employee's responsibility** to refer to the pertinent regulations.

20 Further, the Ordinance on Placement of Visual Display Units ("Bildschirmplatzverordnung") applies, so that the **employer, for example, must cover the burden**

of providing an ergonomic, structurally stable chair, sufficient lighting or a flicker-free computer monitor.

21 With a home office, as opposed to telecommuting, the residential workspace is **not a workplace in the legal sense** put forth in the German Workplace Ordinance, which regulates such matters. According to this regulation, the employer does **not have a right of disposal or use of the employee's residence** or any part of it; therefore the residence is not subject to falling under the meaning of company premises set forth in the Workplace Ordinance and the law generally has no application to a Home Office. Off-site work locations (with the exception of construction sites) are also excluded from the enforcement of the Workplace Ordinance.

22 So long as the work from the office is only occasional, there is usually no need to stipulate the home office usage in a **home lease agreement** for the approval of a third party, as the usage of the home as a work space is only an exception and, because of this, the overall impression of the space being used as living space, as stated in many standard German leases, is not overstepped. If the home office becomes a more regular workplace, it needs to be clarified when needed in what **ownership status** you are in and whether the usage of the agreement/relationship with the owner/leaser allows for agreement on the living space being used as workplace.

Question 138
Should the employer's right to access be stipulated?

Answer

23 No, due to the **exceptional nature** of a home office, an agreement to allow the employer access for the purpose of establishing a home office, an eventual exchange of company work equipment, resolving of problems or checking if the residential work space conforms with legal requirements is **principally not required**. It is in every case worth thinking about this if the residential work space is to be used for a set period of time and not just temporarily and occasionally. The same applies for the possible granting of access to works council members.

Question 139
What costs need to be considered when setting up a home office?

Answer

24 What **technical work equipment** the employee will need to be equipped with and **who is responsible for the purchase** and maintenance should be regulated in the agreement to establish a home office. Generally speaking, the increasing costs cannot be extensive, since the relocation of the workplace in a home is only temporary. What needs to be considered here is:

- the extent of the furnishings of the employee with computer, laptop, monitor, landline, printer, scanner, fax machine;
- Intranet access;
- usage of private printer, internet and telephone connections;
- providing of a mobile phone;
- exclusion of allocating additional work equipment that goes beyond the named or commonly used work equipment;
- (partially) no assuming of cost that arise from working from home (e.g. energy, heat, etc.);
- no assuming of travel cost for travel from the home to the company;
- if applicable, the private usage of work equipment.

Question 140

What considerations need to be made with respect to non-disclosure requirement and data protection?

Answer

Because of the home office being in the employee's home, a home office always runs 25
the risk that **third parties** (e.g. partners/spouses, children, tenants, handymen of guests of the employee) could gain access to the residential work space and therefore to company work equipment (i.e. computer or laptop) and, consequently, company of **business secrets**. It is therefore of particular interest to the employer to ensure that the employee carries the burden of preventing third parties access of this information. This applies also to safe keeping of records, files, data mediums, as well as the secure disposal of confidential documents, work papers, etc. The employer should instruct the employee that all **usage by third parties is strictly prohibited** and that data protection rules – like quality of work assurances – that would apply at the company work site also apply to the residentially situated work place.

Question 141

With regard to time, how is the availability of the employee to be handled?

Answer

As a rule employees working out of a home office are free to **independently organ-** 26
ize his/her work space. This applies to working time models like flextime anyway. While the employee is still integrated into the employer's organization, **core hours** during which the employee will be available to his/her co-workers should be agreed to in order to maintain organizational working time uniformity. The employee should be **principally free to arrange his/her work from a home office** within

the framework of company rules. For extra work or overtime, rules that differ from the those that apply to the company work site should not find application.

Question 142
What needs to be considered for a home office with regard to adherence of the German Working Hours Act?

Answer
27 The German Working Hours Act also applies employees working out of a home office. Employers are **principally responsible for adherence** to the law's provisions. Since checking on whether or not these rules are being adhered to is nearly impossible, it needs to be put in writing that the obligation to adhere to the law is **delegated to the employee**. Here, this corresponds with the duty in respect of care and supervision the employer carries to ensure that the employee is aware of this obligation and also has the necessary knowledge relating to the respective legal provisions. In doing this, the documenting of work performed from the residential work place is handed over to the employee.

Question 143
Is the employer's right to withdraw from permitting a home office required when such a working arrangement is initially established?

Answer
28 The employer should reserve his/her **right of cancellation** in case the employee demonstrates that he/she is not suitable for working out of a home office. The principles found in the Act Governing General Rules and Conditions ("AGB") are to be considered if the home office option is **set forth in an individual contractual agreement** with the employer or in the form of a **unilateral employer guideline.** This applies in particular for sec. 308, no. 4 of the German Civil Code, which is intended for this right to make amendments ("Änderungsvorbehalt"). Accordingly, the agreement on a right by the employer to modify the benefit promised or deviate from it is invalid, if the agreement of the modification or deviation is **unreasonable for the employee**, taking the employer's interests into account. The relevant case law about sec. 308 of the German Civil Code informs us that the right of revocation, in case the benefit is revoked, is seen as reasonable if the employee can recognize the grounds made use of his right of revocation. The immediate disclosure of the grounds for the revocation is therefore to be in the home office agreement. Other rules apply only to home office agreements by way of a works agreements, since the content control of the General Business Terms according to the German Civil Code do not find application to works agreements.

The right of revocation with a revocation period should be agreed upon, so that both parties can **be prepared for a possible ending** of the opportunity of home office usage. In this case a **deadline of one month** is seen as sufficient, since the option to work out of home office is only temporary anyway. 29

Question 144

What needs to be considered when the home office arrangement is established by a works agreement?

Answer

The institution of home office regulations can also be a topic of a voluntary works agreement. The advantage of a works agreement is, firstly, that a single, uniform **set of rules is created** and, secondly, that **no commitment to strict legal provisions** of the Act Governing General Business Conditions exists. This is not applicable to works and service agreements, in accordance with the sec. 310 of the German Civil Code. 30

In **special situations**, the mandatory participation of employees **can come under consideration** depending on the regulatory content of the agreement. This is definitely the case if home offices are an option for multiple employees of groups of employees; the working hours are fixed company-wide, especially, for example, if **a special, set timeframe** is established for home offices. However, if employees who have a home office are allowed to set their own hours, the participation of all employees in that decision per the German Works Constitution Act is to be denied. If, however, there is a framework for a self-determination of home office with regard to working times, the German Works Constitution Act can infringe upon the right depending on the situation. 31

If the employer wants to **survey the employees in advance**, the co-determination rights of the works council are to be borne in mind in so far as the home office comes into account. 32

There is **no mandatory right of co-determination** if the regular working times set forth in the German Works Constitution Act ("Betriebsverfassungsgesetz") apply to home offices. The same applies if, for example, only a small number of employees are affected, as the required collective basis for co-determination rights is missing. 33

The German Works Constitution Act informs us that the works council enjoys a **comprehensive right to consult** ("Unterrichtungsrecht") by the carrying out of their rights. This lends itself to regularly inform the works council about the status of home office positions (number or employees, regularity of use). Beyond that the timekeeping records are to be made available to the works council in accordance with the usual company regulations. 34

Chapter 12 Illness | Krankheit

! **Definition, Legal Principles**
When ill, employees are entitled to **continued remuneration for up to six months** according to German law. Collective bargaining agreements can deviate from this and provide for a longer time. The average number of days lost due to illness for 2012 by those in the state health care system was 3.64%. This works out to about 14 days missed. There has been a noticeable increase in sick days taken over the last few years. Illness-related days taken should be reported to the employer without delay, not least those taken due to work environment and trust.

Question 145
Does the employee have to notify the employer of his/her illness?

Answer
1 German law mandates that employees who are ill have to notify the employer of illness **without undue delay**. A telephone call suffices to serve this and so long as nothing to the contrary has been agreed upon by the two parties. If the illness causes an inability to work for more than three days, the employee has to provide the employer with a **doctor's note or certificate of inability** to work by no later than the fourth day the employee is out due to illness. However, the employer may request a certificate of inability to work as early as the first day out of the office. This right of the employer is not within the unbound discretion of the employer. It is not especially necessary, for example, that there is an accusation against the employee that he/she has previously only faked an illness.

Question 146
What is a certificate of inability to work ("Arbeitsunfähigkeitsbescheinigung")?

Answer
2 The German "certificate of inability to work" is **more than a sick note**; it is a certificate from a licensed physician that names the person and provides the **length of time** that person will be out ill and unable to work.

Question 147
What applies to foreign certificates of inability to work?

Answer
3 Foreign certificates of this nature principally have come to possess the same evidentiary value as a domestic certificate of inability to work. What is required is that the foreign certificate is actually **a certificate of inability to work** and is not a mere sick note.

Question 148
Does the employee have to tell the employer about the precise illness?

Answer
Generally not. Such a notification requirement exists only if the employer has a justifiable reason to know what the diagnosis is. An example of such a justification would be when the cause for one person being unable to work becomes an issue where the employer has to take **safety measures to protect other employees**, has influence on the obligation to continue paying wages or because someone else has been injured by it. 4

Question 149
Does the employer have to pay the employee if he is ill?

Answer
Yes, the employer is obligated to continue paying wages **for the first six weeks** of the employee's inability to work. Afterward the health insurance and state social security comes into effect. Alone the burden of continuing to pay the employee does not entitle the employer to give the employee notice of termination due to illness. 5

Question 150
What rules apply to long-term illnesses?

Answer
An illness is long-term if the employee is rendered unable to work at the capacity he/she is expected to as a result of the illness. To meet this standard, the employee's inability to work has to be for **a period of approximately 1.5 years.** 6

A long-term illness may justify an ordinary dismissal so long as the recovery cannot be projected. However, this is a rare case in Germany. 7

Question 151
What applies to repeated illness(es)?

Answer
What is decisive here is whether the inability to work is based on a new illness or the same one. If the repeated inability to work is based on another illness, the employee has an unrestricted entitlement to continued compensation. 8

On the other hand, **if the same illness is the cause** of the inability to work, the employer only has an obligation to continue to pay wages if the time missed due to the same illness does not exceed six weeks within no more than a **six-month pe-** 9

riod. The employer still has to continue to pay wages as well if twelve months elapse between the first incidence of the employee's inability to work and the new period during of his/her inability to work.

Question 152
Can the employer have the employee commit to preventative medical care or rehabilitation measures?

Answer
10 No, but different rules may apply to certain business sectors and particular jobs. In those sectors, a **medical check-up** can be set as a mandatory condition for service, such as for pilots.

Question 153
Does the employer have to cover the costs for the employee's treatment?

Answer
11 No, the payer of preventative medical care and rehabilitation measures are:
- the German Federal Employment Agency;
- Health Insurers;
- accident or worker's compensation insurance;
- war victim assistance carriers;
- public-sector youth worker welfare carriers, and
- the statutory health insurance system.

Question 154
Does the employer have to provide precautionary measures, e.g. vaccinations, training to minimize back pain, eye exams, provide a company gym, dietary counseling, etc.?

Answer
12 Beyond the usual facilities and furnishings of the workplace, no requirement of the employer to provide precautionary measures exist. However, if the employee is declared to be unable to work for more than six weeks within a one-year period, the employer is obligated to **attempt preventing the employee** from getting a renewed illness of the same sort (e.g. by improving the work environment).

Question 155
What happens if the employee had a work-related accident?

Answer

If an accident takes place on the premises of the workplace, a **company-approved physician** must be consulted. The chosen physician has to have been approved by the trade association, specializing in work and commuting-related accidents. Further, the employer and the physician performing treatment has to report the accident to the employer's liability insurance company using a special form. 13

Question 156

What happens if the employee gets into an accident on the way to or from work that makes that employee unable to work?

Answer

14 A workplace accident is a situation for the statutorily mandated **accident insurance.** It is to be differentiated from pure free-time activities, sports and non-work-related driving accidents (insured activities). If the employee is injured on his way from home to his/her workplace, he/she is insured. Such injuries are defined as being ones that take place on the way to or from the workplace ("Wegeunfälle"). They are a sub-form of **workplace accidents**. They are conditioned on an interrelationship between the insured activity and the distance covered. It is of influence to insurance coverage that the injured person took **the most direct route**. Of immediate importance in such a case is that the injured person freely chose the shortest option in time or distance, as well as which mode of transportation was to be used.

15 Should the injured person have, for example, taken an **alternate route/short cut**, the injury is not covered by insurance unless it is of minimal significance. There are therefore alternate routes expressly permitted by law; e.g. picking up a carpool participant or transporting children to a daycare or childcare giver.

Question 157

What happens if a third party caused the accident leading to the employee's inability to work?

Answer

16 If a third party caused an employee's inability to work, the injured employee has a right to **collect damages from that third party** who cased it. This claim to damages includes reimbursement for lost wages. Since the employer is obligated to continue paying wages for a six-week period, German law provides that there be **no loss of wages** for the employee who is rendered unable to work. The employee's claim against the liable party (tortfeasor) is transferred in this respect to the employer. The employee is obligated to furnish the given employer with the information required to assert these rights.

Question 158

May the employee pursue secondary employment during the time he/she is out?

Answer

17 No, the employee may not pursue secondary employment during the time which he/she is out because of illness or injury so long as it can **harm the process of healing** or getting better. If the employee violates this rule, he/she may be reprimanded.[1]

Question 159

May the employee do yard work, gardening, or sports during the time he/she is out?

Answer

18 The employee has to commit him/herself to **"health-enhancing" behavior**. Whether the employee's behavior is enhancing health or not must be determined on a case-by-case basis, as everyone is different. In certain cases, as with mental illnesses, for example, gardening can be seen as promoting health and would therefore be permitted. But, if the employee has a flu-like illness which renders him/her bed-ridden, gardening would, of course, be forbidden.

1 See Chapter 6.

Chapter 13 Job interview | Bewerbungsgespräch

Definition, Legal Principles

An interview serves as a way for both applicant and employer **to become acquainted** and **for comparison of expectations**. If the employer insists upon an interview, he/she is expected to cover the travel costs (e.g. transportation and sustenance). As a part of the interview process, the employer has a right to ask the applicant specific questions. However, the scope of his right is not limitless. Should the applicant be asked an **impermissible question**, he/she has the so-called **"right to lie"**. Due to the burden of proof, two individuals representing the employer should be present at the interview and the content of the discussion should be recorded. In order to get the interview started, it is common to ask the applicant to briefly introduce him/herself at the outset. The talk is generally marked by a flexible approach, one which allows for the possibility of putting forth certain main points.

Question 160

May the employer "google" an applicant or perform a search on the applicant on social networking sites?

Answer

There is no general ban on this. However, a search would represent **data collection.** 1
According to the German Data Protection Act ("Bundesdatenschutzgesetz – BDSG") only certain "*personal data may be collected, processed or used for employment-related purposes where necessary for hiring decisions or, after hiring, for carrying out or terminating the employment contract.*"

Question 161

What questions is the employee not required to answer?

Answer

Questions that may not be asked include those that are about employees 2

- political party,
- handicap,
- marital status,
- pregnancy or desire to have children,
- reason(s) for leaving a prior employer,
- whether someone holds public office, honorary or elected,
- club, association or organization membership(s),
- religious affiliation,
- previous criminal convictions,
- union membership, or
- financial situation.

Question 162
May the employee remain silent on such points?

Answer
3 Yes.

Question 163
What happens if the employee provides a false answer?

Answer
4 It depends. Employees may answer questions of a discriminatory nature falsely, and employers cannot fire the employee for doing so. Some of the topics in this respect include issues related to pregnancy or disabilities. With matters such as prior criminal convictions, whether or not an employer has a justifiable interest depends, and a **balancing of interests** must be undertaken. Employers may nevertheless dispute the validity of or end an employment relationship for misstatements.

Question 164
May the employer ask the applicant if he/she has a criminal record?

Answer
5 The employer may ask about the applicant's criminal record insofar as it is **of importance to entering into and the proper implementation of the employment relationship**. Some examples of crimes of particular relevance to labor law are fraudulent acts for cashiers or tellers, or traffic violations for drivers (e.g. taxi, limo, bus, etc.).

Question 165
May the employer demand that the applicant submits to a background check?

Answer
6 Proof of a criminal background check is often referred to as a "certificate of good behavior" ("Führungszeugnis") by Germans, and an employer may demand it be provided **in special circumstances**, such as for security-related fields or public service.

Question 166
May the employer demand that a credit check by the German Credit Bureau ("SCHUFA-Auskunft") be provided?

Answer

Such checks are not allowed. Reason: SCHUFA credit checks also contain information about private finances, and this information could lead to allowing conclusions to be drawn about how the applicant leads his/her life. This sort of information is **of no relevance to the employer**. Further, it impermissibly forces the applicant to nearly fully disclose his/her private life situation and lifestyle. 7

Question 167

May the employer ask the applicant's former employer about the applicant?

Answer

The principles on the right to ask questions determine whether asking a former or current employer is permissible. Consequently, such inquiries are **only allowed with the permission of the applicant**. 8

Question 168

May the employer ask the applicant about the applicant's records in the central federal traffic register at Central German Federal Vehicle Registration Authority ("Kraftfahrtbundesamt")?

Answer

No, because the German central federal traffic register's records do not deal with criminal offenses. Other rules would apply if the job applied for would require it, such as applying for a job as a driver. 9

Question 169

Does the applicant have to undergo a physical exam?

Answer

The question of physical exam's permissibility **depends on the position to be filled**, whereas the scope of the examination expands with the potential for danger presented by the position applied for. Sight and responsiveness exams for pilots or color-blindness for printers are permissible. Comprehensive personality analysis and personality and intelligence tests are impermissible. 10

Question 170

May the employer demand a certificate of good health?

Answer

11 The employer may demand a certificate of good health only if **required for a special job**. These jobs are named in the German Infection Protection Act ("Infektionsschutzgesetz"). Some examples are workers

- who come into contact with food,
- in medical and nursing fields, or
- preschool teachers.

Chapter 14 Labor Unions | Gewerkschaften

Definition, Legal Principles
Labor Unions are the democratic joining of employees for the purpose of maintaining and improving working conditions. Membership in a labor union is **voluntary**. With unions in many other places in the world, German labor unions set out to achieve the following goals: better working times, increased wages and better working conditions in general. As part of collective bargaining agreements, labor unions negotiate certain conditions and provisions with employers and in this way balance existing differences in power between the weaker employee and the stronger employer. In Germany there are currently 137 labor unions and 68,000 collective bargaining agreements registered with German authorities which are deemed to be valid agreements. Operating as an **umbrella organization**, the Confederation of German Trade Unions ("Deutscher Gewerkschaftsbund – DGB") has eight, individual unions as members, including IG Metall, ver.di and the Police Union. In 2012 the number of union members in Germany reached 6.1 million workers, with IG Metall currently being Germany's largest union with approximately 2.25 million members. Additionally, there is the German Civil Service Federation ("dbb"), the National Federation of Christian Trade Union and other unions that reach across other sectors, such as the health care services, other public service branches, service sectors and airline and airport services.

Question 171
What is a labor union under German Law?

Answer
A labor union is a democratic union of workers that voluntarily join their economic 1
and social interests together to form a representative body.

Question 172
What is the meaning of the "industrial principle" ("Industrieprinzip")?

Answer
The "Industrieprinzip" signifies that all employees in a given branch are **joined to-** 2
gether in one labor union. This has the advantage that only one labor union is responsible for the company and the employer does not have to negotiate with more than one labor union simultaneously. However, in some industry sectors two or more unions were formed due to historical or other reasons (for example German railway and pilots).

Question 173
What is the task of a labor union?

Answer
The task of a labor union is **representing the interests of their members** in their 3
capacity as employees. They have to be willing to conclude and oversee collective

bargaining agreements, carry out the process of getting members and offer members advice and lead the representation of members in legal proceedings as well as in industrial dispute actions.

Question 174

May a labor union advertise itself on company premises?

Answer

4 Yes, because there is the constitutional guaranty of freedom of association in Germany ("Koalitionsfreiheit") from which arises the right of the labor union to recruit members at the workplace. Both the unionized employees and the union representatives may distribute informational materials at the workplace and **promote the labor union** itself. They must make sure, however, that their activities do not disturb operations or peace in the workplace.

Question 175

May the employer ask an employee about union membership?

Answer

5 No, but an exception exists if the employer needs the information in order to be able to check collective bargaining coverage.

Question 176

What rights does a labor union have?

Answer

6 Labor unions are granted **initiative, participatory, advisory, and monitoring rights** by the German Works Constitution Act. It is a matter of rights in relation to the orderly establishment of a works council, youth worker and trainee representation, the monitoring of the orderly execution of the German Works Constitution Act via employer and works council, the advisory participation in conferences and meetings, and the general cooperation of the employer with the works council for the welfare of company employees. Furthermore, the labor union is entitled to conclude collective bargaining agreements and to carry out strikes (industrial disputes).[1]

1 See Chapter 14 for further information.

Question 177

Does the employer have to allow union members entrance into the company?

Answer

Yes, union representatives are entitled the right of access for the performance of the 7
union's special tasks, a power assigned to them by the German Works Constitution Act. Unless an overriding need of operations, essential security regulations or protection of company secrets conflicts with this right of access, these rights have legal force and must be observed.

Chapter 15 M&A Transfer of Business | M&A Betriebsübergang

! **Definition, Legal Principles**

Section 613a was inserted into the German Civil Code ("BGB") in 1972. Its current form is due to European Community Council Directive 77/187/EC of February 2, 1977 for the alignment of member states' legal regulations regarding the protection of employee rights in the transfer of business ventures, companies or parts of companies. Thus, the statutory provisions of the German Civil Code are to be seen **in connection with EC Directives.** An alignment of Section 613a of the German Civil Code took place in 1980 with the Act Modifying the German Labor Law in Accordance with the European Community Labor Law ("EG-Anpassungsgesetz"). Due to this dependence on secondary European Community legislation, Section 613a of the German Civil Code is to be **interpreted in accordance with EU law in case of doubt.** By law, Section 613a of the German Civil Code regulates a succession to specific rights and obligations that are foreign to the German Civil Code.

Condition for a transfer of business is that a company or part of a **company changes ownership** by a legal transaction. This can take place via sale, lease, dividing of the company or merger. The sense and purpose of the statutory requirements of section 613a is complete protection of employees. For that reason, a transfer of business does not lead to the end of the **employment relationship.** Rather, that very relationship moves over by law to the new company. The rights and obligations of the new employer remain the same as the previous one. Section 613a therefore plays a pivotal role in these transactions, and the details are numerous and complicated. For this reason, section 613a of the German Civil Code is regularly matter for European Court of Justice case law and is impacted by extensive German Labor Court case law.

Question 178
What is a transfer of business?

Answer
1 A transfer of business, or successorship, is a legal change of ownership of a business or part of a business by way of a **legal agreement**, through which the employment relationship of the employee transfers to the new proprietor if there is a failure to object.

Question 179
What are the legal consequences of a transfer of business?

Answer
2 The new proprietor has to **adopt all conditions** that existed at the time the employees are transferred to the new business. Collective bargaining agreements and works agreements continue to operate as individual contracts unless collective bargaining agreement with other rules apply to business of the new company or the business/businesses part remains as it is.

Question 180
What is the legal status of the transferee?

Answer
The transferee enters into an employment relationship with all of its rights and responsibilities. He/she is further **responsible for remaining employee claims**, such as bonuses and pension entitlements. 3

Question 181
Is the transfer of business subject to consultation or agreement of the works council?

Answer
No, the transfer of the business as such is not subject to co-determination of the employees. That said, the works council **can have a right of participation** if the business succession is connected to considerable disadvantages of at least part of the workforce. 4

Question 182
What is the legal status of the previous employer?

Answer
With the transfer of business, the employment relationship to the previous employer ends. The previous employer is only liable for retirement relationship claims and those arising out of vested pension claims by former employees. Along with the new employer, the previous employer is jointly and severally **liable for the outstanding claims** arising from the employment relationship that were incurred prior to the transfer of business (i.e. wages) and that have become due **no more than one year** after said transfer. 5

Question 183
Can employees contest the transfer of business?

Answer
Yes, **employees can legally contest** the transfer of business. Other rules apply in cases of company mergers, as the previous employer legally ceases to exist in this instance. 6

Question 184
For how long can the employee legally contest the transfer of his/her employment relationship?

Answer
7 The employee can contest the transfer of business **within a month** following the receipt of a legally valid written notification. In cases where there is a failure to notify or the notification employees receive is erred, they can indefinitely object to the transfer of business so long as they have not forfeit their rights.

Question 185
With whom does the employee have to lodge his objection about a transfer of business?

Answer
8 Either the **previous employer** or **new proprietor** may be the legal recipient of an objection to the transfer of business.

Question 186
What are the consequences of the objection?

Answer
9 If the employee uses his/her rights to object, the employment relations with the former employer remains.

Question 187
What is a letter of notification in this context ("Unterrichtungsschreiben")?

Answer
10 The letter of notification is **legally recognized**. It represents an information and knowledge base of the employee for carrying out of his/her right to objection. It informs the employee about the transfer of business and the additional legal consequences for him/her, the company and applicable legal standards and informs the employee about his/her **right of revocation**.

Question 188
When does the notification of the transfer of business need to go out?

Answer

There is no law regulating the time at which the notification has to go out. The notification can go out before, at the time of or after the transfer of business. 11

Question 189

Who has to provide the notification?

Answer

The previous employer and the new owner are obligated to provide the notification. 12
They can provide that notification either **jointly or separately**.

Question 190

Who has to be notified?

Answer

All **employees that are affected by the transfer of business** have to be notified. 13
This includes those in partial retirement, but not retirees.

Question 191

What has to be included in the letter of notification?

Answer

The contents of the letter of notification contains the following **4-point catalog**: 14

1. time or planned time of the transfer of business;
2. the reason for the transfer of business;
3. the legal, commercial and social consequences the transfer of business has for employees; and
4. envisaged measures that concern employees.

The details are continuously substantiated by the German Federal Labor Court and the 15
European Court of Justice. Thus, the **case law** on the matter is quite comprehensive.

Question 192

Does the notification have to be in writing?

Answer

Yes, **written form** is the intended one by law. It is possible to convey the em- 16
ployee's letters of notification by e-mail, internet, photocopy, or fax.

Question 193
Who has to sign the letter of notification?

Answer
17 The written-form requirement does not make a signature necessary. However, either by replication of his/her signature or in some other manner, the individual conveying the notification (the previous employer or the new proprietor) has to **make the author of the letter discernible** at the end of it.

Question 194
What happens if the written letter of notification does not come or is erred?

Answer
18 The letter of notification represents a **legal obligation.** As such, the employer makes him/herself open to civil action if that employer fails to provide a letter of notification or provide one that is erred. Further, the clock for the **one-month time limit** the employee has to exercise his/her right to object would not begin.

Chapter 16 Minijob | Geringfügige Beschäftigung

Definition, Legal Principles

Marginal employment – the minijob – is gaining increasing attention on the German job market, not to mention **international attention.** In February 2012 there were in fact about 7.45 million people working in minjobs in Germany, so-called "minijobbers". This form of employment relationship gives **additional income** to people who are not in the position with their primary job to make a living. In addition those who are professionally less competitive in particular often find minijobs as a **way to enter the job market.**

Minijobs are arranged in two ways:

- nominally paid positions with a remuneration of up to 450 € or
- short-term employment that is limited to no more than two months or 50 workdays in a given calendar year, as explained in the German Social Security Code.

From an employment law perspective both forms of minijobs refer to a full-fledged employment relationship with its rights and obligations.

Question 195

Do minijobs require a written contract?

Answer

No, as generally a minijob employment contract – like any other employment contract in Germany – can be concluded orally; the written form is **not required by law**. However, the employer has to bear sec. 2 of the Documentation of Essential Employment Conditions Act ("Nachweisgesetz") in mind; it states that employers have **no more than one month** following the agreed upon start of an employee's employment relationship to **put the important conditions of employment in writing** and hand them to the employee. An employer not complying with this stipulation can find him/herself in difficulties should there be disputes. 1

It is very important for employers to note that if it is decided that the employment relationship is **term-limited** and that agreement is **not put into writing**, a **permanent employment relationship exists** under German law. 2

Question 196

What applies in terms of remuneration, e.g. special payments?

Answer

Those who are marginally employed may **not be treated worse** than other employees, be it in terms of normal pay rates or with benefits-in-kind. In this context, the right to remuneration and benefits-in-kind is in line with the amount that a full-timer would earn for that number of hours. In the same vain the marginally em- 3 ployed are also entitled to the **same special payments** – such as Christmas bonuses – that are paid to full-time employees.

Question 197
Are "minijobbers" entitled to vacation?

Answer
4 Yes, someone who is marginally employed has the **same right to the minimum vacation time** set forth in the Federal Paid Leave Act as any other employee. That amount of time is, given a 6-day work week, 24 working days per calendar year. If a different distribution of working days applies to the particular employee, the number of vacation days **is to be calculated** correspondingly.[1]

5 The right to vacation time is not recognized, however, until the minijob employee has worked for the employer for **six consecutive months.** The amount of vacation entitlement can result from a collective bargaining agreement, company practice or employment contract.

Question 198
What rules apply to the marginally employed for sick days or holidays?

Answer
6 If a marginally employed person takes ill and is unable to work for that reason, he/she is entitled to have 100% of regular salary **continued to be paid for the time out of work** once that person has worked **four consecutive weeks** for the company. The entitlement is limited to six weeks. If the inability to work lasts longer than six weeks, the "minijobber" has a **right to sick pay** from his/her health insurer.

7 The same applies with holidays for "minijobbers": they are **entitled to continuation of pay** on holidays according to German law. However, unlike being out sick, this right exists **from the first day** of the employment relationship.

Question 199
Are minijobbers allowed to work other jobs at the same time as the minijob?

1 See Chapter 35.

Answer

No, a marginally employed person is also **prohibited from engaging in business activities** that compete with the employer during the legal existence of the employment relationship without individual or collective agreement rules to the contrary. 8

An exception exists if the secondary employment involves a **merely simple job** that could at most lead to a subordinate form of support to a competitor firm and, apart from that, **does not impact the employer's interests**. This especially applies if the employee solely works a part-time job and is for that reason advised to work another job in order to support him/herself. 9

Question 200

How is the employment relationship of a "minijobber" ended?

Answer

Because marginal employment nevertheless represents a full-fledged employment relationship under German law, **no special rules** apply with respect to the ending of the "minjobber's" employment relationship.[2] 10

Question 201

Do different rules with respect to works council elections apply to those working "minijobs"?

Answer

No; since the marginally employed are part-timers as a rule and are also company employees. In other words, there are **no special rules** for them in this respect. The marginally employed **can vote** in works council elections and **can run for office** should they wish. 11

---

2 See also Chapter 7.

Chapter 17 Miscellaneous | Sonstiges

Question 202
What taxation and social insurance reporting requirements exist for the employer in Germany?

Answer
1 German law requires that the employer report the employment of workers to the responsible **social insurance carrier**. The employer is further obligated to report income tax withholdings.

Question 203
Which documents does the employer have to provide to the employee during the employment relationship?

Answer
2 Due to a secondary obligation derived from German Employment Law, the employer must also provide a statement of income and the issuance of documentation for the application of parental-leave allowance. Where there is a valid reason, the employer is to provide an interim performance review. A valid reason could be, for example, a change of supervisor or in the goal to complete his/her application records for an upcoming application process. Additionally, the employer has the duty to hand out an **electronic income tax certificate** (the USA equivalent being a W2).

Question 204
What is understood by the expression "working papers" ("Arbeitspapiere") in Germany?

Answer
3 Working papers denote the **entirety of papers and documents** that the employer hands out to the employee at the end of the employment relationship. These are, for example, report of taken holidays, social security ID, income tax certificate ("Lohnsteuerbescheinigung"), etc.

Question 205
Does the employer have to keep personnel files?

Answer

Only in civil service law does a legal duty to keep personnel files exist in Germany. 4
However, should the employer create personnel files, he/she is obligated to treat them as **confidential**. The employee has the right to see his/her personnel file. Additionally, the employer is obligated to keep the records in a manner that accords with German tax and social security regulations. The records are especially important in cases where the company is subject to an **external audit**.

Question 206

What is a company custom ("betriebliche Übung") understood to be in Germany?

Answer

A company practice indicates the fact that an employee can conclude from regular 5
repetition of certain conduct by the given employer how the employer will reasonably be **expected to act in the future**. That would be adopted, for example, in cases where a practice has been repeated by the employer three times without expressing the reservation of the practice's voluntary nature. This applies, for instance, to the granting of bonuses and fringe benefits, extra days off (e.g. December 24th and 31st). The consequence of a company custom is that the voluntary performance of certain customs on the part of the employer **will become obligatory ones**.

Chapter 18 Part Time | Teilzeit

Definition, Legal Principles
While the number of full-time employees in Germany has been decreasing, the number of part-timers has been steadily increasing. Every employee has a **right to reduce or redistribute working hours** according to sec. 8 of the Part-time Work and Fixed-term Employment Contracts Act ("Teilzeit- und Befristungsgesetz"). To begin, part-time employees cannot be treated worse than their full-time counterparts. For this reason, additional benefits such as Christmas bonuses have to be proportionally paid out to part-timers as well.

Question 207
Are full-time employees entitled to part-time work?

Answer
1 Yes, but a requirement for this is that the employee has been working for the given employer for at least six months. Additionally, a **request for part-time work can only be made biennially**.

Question 208
What has to be in an application for part-time work?

Answer
2 A general requirement is that the request be formulated in a way that allows the employer to **reply with a simple "yes"**. What the request has to make very clear is that the employee wishes to work reduced working hours and the scope of those hours.

Question 209
Does the request need to be made in writing?

Answer
3 No, as the law makes no such requirement. The request should nevertheless be put in writing in order to **provide a paper trail** should one be needed.

Question 210
When can the employer refuse part-time work?

Answer
4 If the employer does not wish to approve the request for part-time work, he/she has to be able to counter with rational, imaginable operational reason. As a rule, there

are **sufficiently serious grounds to deny part-time work** if the reduced working hours considerably impair the organization, work flow or security in the workplace, or bring about disproportionate costs.

Question 211
How far in advance does the employee have to submit his/her part-time work request?

Answer
This has to be done **at least three months prior** to when the employee wishes to 5
invoke his/her right to working part-time.

Question 212
When does the employer have to decide on a part-time work request?

Answer
The employer has to inform the employee about whether the requested period for 6
part-time work has been agreed to **no later than one month** before that time period commences. Should the employer fail to do this, the working times the employee requested will be granted automatically.

Question 213
Does every company have to allow for part-time hours?

Answer
No. The right to part-time exists only if the employer employs at least 15 employees. 7

Question 214
How are the 15 employees counted?

Answer
All employees who regularly work for the given employer are to be counted, regard- 8
less of the number of hours the employee works. Trainees are not counted. Temporary employees are to be counted if they work regularly for the employer. Basically, a **per capita principle** is applied so that even marginally employed persons are counted.

Question 215
What happens if the employer denies the request for part-time work?

Answer
9 In such a case, the employee would have the right to take his case to court. What comes into consideration is an **action for performance**, namely, the consent to change an existing employment contract. However, this does not entitle the employee to be absent from work.

Question 216
What points should definitely be stipulated in a part-time employment agreement?

Answer
10 The following should definitely be stipulated:
- weekly working times/days,
- the concrete work obligations,
- compensation,
- vacation time,
- the proportionate workload reduction,
- probationary period,
- confidentiality obligations,
- company rules and collective wage agreements,
- the saving clause (a clause that, among other things, provides that the rest of an agreement will not become invalid if one part does).

Question 217
Is the general entitlement to part-time the only means for reducing working hours?

Answer
11 No, since, beyond the general entitlement to part-time work, there are also **special legal provisions** granting a decrease in working hours for certain employees. These groups include parents during the duration of their **parental leave** or employees who have to look after relatives in need of **nursing care**.

Question 218
Is there a right to part-time work after the conclusion of agreed upon parental leave ends?

Answer

In principle, the employment relationship is **revived after parental leave** ends. 12
This depends on if the parent in question had worked part-time during the parental leave or not. Accordingly, employees can assert a right to working part-time after their parental leave ends.

Question 219

After parental leave ends, does the employee have to be back to work full-time again for six months before he/she can request part-time hours from the employer?

Answer

If the employment relationship has existed already for six months, the employee 13
can submit a request to work part-time work after parental leave has ended. Parental leave is **calculated as time employed**, since the employment relationship continued during this period. What one must watch out for is that he/she adheres to the **three-month deadline** for submitting the timeframe for part-time work.

Question 220

How is the vacation time of part-timers calculated?

Answer

The problem with calculating vacation time often arises if flexible work hours were 14
agreed to and the range of hours per day worked varies. Here, the first thing to be calculated is how many days the employee works at the company on average. The nominal amount of vacation days for a full-time employee, multiplied by the actual number of days worked by an employee working part-time during a specific number of working days that set the base period, divided by the number of working days for a full-time employee during the set base period.

Question 221

How does part-time employment end?

Answer

It can end in one of two ways: **termination of employment** or a **change in con-** 15
tract. With termination of the employment relationship, through a severance agreement, it can be ended with notice or via the conclusion of a valid fixed-term. Further, part-time work can be ended with mutually agree upon change to the contract.

Question 222

Does an employee have a right to return to full-time work after a having worked reduced hours?

Answer

16 As a rule, there is no right for an employee to return to the same job after having worked in a part-time capacity. However, all employees working part-time who wish to extend their working hours do indeed have a **right to be considered preferentially** by employers for full-time positions indeed.

Chapter 19 Permanent Establishment | Betriebsstätte

Definition, Legal Principles

With a view to globalization, permanent establishments for **companies that operate abroad are increasing in importance.** This especially applies to investments of foreign companies in Germany. In this context the term permanent establishment serves to indicate the regional boundaries and allocation of revenue and sales at home and abroad. More clearly defined, permanent establishments, constructions born out of tax law, are fixed places of business or facilities that serve the carrying out of company business with a certain level of consistency.

That is how the **concept of a permanent establishment** decides on, among other things, whether reduced tax obligations come into play in accordance with national law (income tax laws) or in which state ("Bundesland") profits are subject to VAT. Section 12 of the German Tax Code ("Abgabenordnung") contains a basic definition for permanent establishments for German tax law, according to which a fixed place of business or facility that is required, for a certain period, to serve the business activities of a company and exercises more than a mere temporary power of direction over the taxpayer in order for a permanent establishment to exist. In particular, the following positions are to be seen as permanent establishments in the sense of the German Tax Code:

- subsidiaries,
- places where management is located,
- places of operation or production, and
- warehouses.

Question 223

Can the use of employees in Germany by a foreign company create a tax liability for a company's German income?

Answer

A foreign company's usage of its workers in Germany can lead to taxation of the in- 1
come related to assignment abroad. The workforce usage abroad in Germany can be justified to be the "normal" workplace in the spirit of German Tax Code and the OECD's model treaty on the matter in order to **avoid double taxation** of income. The workforce usage abroad can also take place by placing an employee as a permanent representative in Germany according to the same laws.

If a foreign company makes German income within the context of a so-called 2
representative business establishment ("Vertreterbetriebsstätte") or via a permanent representative, a **reduction of the tax liability** for the foreign company results. The characteristics of the given representative (establishment) are determined by the principles of the German Tax Code, or are regulated in the dual tax treaty with the given foreign country. The tax obligation, as well as the tax exemptions and tax benefits are determined by German Tax Law as well as the dual tax treaty.

Question 224
Under what conditions will a company be liable for taxes by way of workforce usage abroad (permanent representative)?

Answer
3 The conditions for qualifying an employee as a permanent representative are regulated by and included in the German Tax Code:
- person,
- sustainability,
- handling of business operations,
- obligation to follow directives,
- opportunity to conclude contracts/to negotiate contracts/to get clients (sustainable for a company),
- maintenance of the inventory of goods/commodities and their delivery.

4 If these conditions exist, the foreign company with the German income only has a **limited tax liability** due to the function of the permanent representative. This tax obligation can be minimized by German income tax. As a rule, the dual tax treaty regulations for the existence of a permanent representative marginally differ from the national rules of the German tax code and are **often more restrictive**.

5 If the conditions in accordance with terms of the double-taxation treaty are fulfilled and a permanent establishment exists via a permanent representative (fictional permanent establishment ("Betriebsstättenfiktion"), the representative business establishment), the **income of that permanent establishment** in Germany is liable for income and corporate taxes. The obligation to pay commercial tax is tied to the characteristics of the permanent establishment in accordance with the German Tax Code, so that the obligation to pay the tax is to be negated for the permanent representative.

Question 225
Are the conditions the same world-wide?

Answer
6 In an international context, the term "representative business establishment" is based as closely as possible on the representative term found in the OECD model treaty on the avoidance of double taxation; especially Article 5. However, the states that have entered into a **bilateral dual tax treaty agreement** may freely define the term and tax the income from the representative business establishment individually.

Question 226
Which administrative tasks come with the founding of a permanent establishment in Germany?

Answer
In the **business sense**, a permanent settlement in Germany is to inform the local municipality; the municipality itself is to inform the tax office responsible for that municipality. As a rule certificate of registration, the articles of incorporation and shareholder's resolutions of the foreign company as well as the powers of attorney are to be submitted. 7

As with companies situated in Germany, a **book-keeping requirement** in accordance with commercial or tax law can be imposed on the permanent establishment in some instances. Along with that comes the responsibility of noting that there is an obligation of preparing resolutions in accordance with commercial law and disclosing them. 8

Question 227
Does the permanent establishment have to submit a tax declaration?

Answer
In Germany the **principle of world income** ("Welteinkommensprinzip") applies. According to this, entities with limited tax liability are obligated to submit a tax declaration for their domestic (German) income for each source of income. 9

Question 228
Does the employee sent to represent the permanent establishment have the right to negotiate in the name of the foreign company?

Answer
The employee has to be authorized and possess power of attorney. The German term "Vollmacht" (authorized, or be granted power of attorney) is not to be understood in a legal sense here. Through this authorization, the employee receives the **right to negotiate in the name of the foreign company**. 10

Question 229
When is the authority to conclude a contract given?

Answer

11 According to the dual tax treaty's definition of a permanent representative, the right to conclude a contract has to be in a contract that includes the actual job with the company, the one which is usually performed at home. The authorization is usually carried out if the person is authorized to bindingly negotiate all particulars of a contract, including when the contract is signed by another person in the foreign state. The job applies **as it is usually carried out at home** if the contract details are negotiated by the representative but no formal authorization would be given to him or her.

Question 230

Can an employee work for a foreign entity from a home office in Germany without tax-related consequences?

Answer

12 According to the dual tax treaty, the employee establishes a representative permanent establishment as a rule if he/she is working for the foreign company in Germany. Beyond that there is the possibility that the employee establishes a permanent establishment according to the **OECD model agreement**. This would have the consequence of the permanent establishment additionally being **subject to commercial tax.**

Question 231

When does a home office job establish a permanent establishment?

Answer

13 For the existence of a permanent establishment the company has to have a **power of disposition** over the place of business.

14 If the employee rents premises for conducting business activities for an enterprise outside of his own home, those premises may be considered to be at the disposal of the enterprise.

Question 232

What counts as a home office in the home?

Answer

15 The question of whether a staff member's home office in a contracting state established a permanent establishment for a company when in another contracting state is **not discussed in the context of the OECD model agreement** or its commentary.

The OECD taxation committee report of October 12, 2012 suggests that a regularly used and sustained home office is clearly in the company's power of disposition as a basis for the work of the company if, in light of the facts and circumstances, it is obvious that the **company demands that the work is being done from home**. 16

As a consequence, a permanent establishment of the company in the given state would be **created via the home office**. 17

Question 233

For what things is a permanent establishment operating in Germany subject to tax?

Answer

The company in Germany is subject to paying corporate and income taxes on those **profits determined to be those of the permanent establishment**. 18

What is **debatable** is which profits of the representative permanent establishment are to be attributed to them. Theory holds that there is no noteworthy profit attributed to the representative permanent establishment. However, this so-called "Nullsummentheorie" (as in the single-taxpayer approach) is **judged critically by the OECD**. According to the Authorized OECD Approach, the problem is that if the representative permanent establishment's income is carried out in the same way as other types of permanent establishments, the permanent establishment's income – as well as the personal income its representative gains from it – are **subject to tax**. 19

Question 234

How will the permanent establishment's profit be determined?

Answer

The principles about determining a permanent establishment's profit are grounded in Article 7 of the OECD Model Agreement. The overarching "arm's length" principle ("Prinzip des Fremdvergleichs") provides the basis for determining profit, whereas the **profits are attributed to the permanent establishment** if it would have carried out the same or similar work under the same or similar rules under the auspices of an independent company. Along with this the relation to the work between the main office and the permanent establishment, the incurred expenses are also to be considered as if the permanent establishment were to be operating independently of the main office. 20

Practically speaking, the allocation of profits between the main office and the permanent establishment is made in accordance with the decree on permanent establishments ("Betriebsstättenerlass") regarding the direct or indirect method of profit allocation. With the **direct method** the profit is determined severally with 21 reference to the accounting and the methods for determining profits in Germany. With the **indirect method** the entire income of the main office and the permanent establishment's allocation is calculated according to an appropriate formula.

Question 235

What costs are attributable to the permanent establishment?

Answer

22 Due to the arm's length principle, not only the profits but also the costs incurred that arise from the permanent establishment are attributable to it. More specifically, the **attributable costs** include the management and general administrative costs that the main office accrues for the permanent establishment regardless of where the costs are incurred.

Question 236

What has to be documented?

Answer

23 There is an obligation for the taxpayer to cooperate, and that obligation is reflected in the documentation of the business relations with other countries, especially with the main office or permanent establishment. In this respect evidence of the arm's length is to be given by way of **sufficient documentation.**

Question 237

How do the internal performance allocations have to be documented?

Answer

24 In practice the allocation of profit is guaranteed by **keeping separate records of accounting books** for the permanent establishment, and on that basis the permanent establishment's attributable profits are reported.

25 Regarding the documentation of the internal performance allocation of the permanent establishment, it is to be approached in two steps with respect to the OECD's 2010 "Transfer Pricing Guidelines for Multinational Enterprises and Tax Administrations". The first step is identifying the activities carried out by the permanent establishment with help of a **functional and actual analysis** (Function and Risk Analysis) in which the economically significant activities and responsibilities of the permanent establishment are reported. The second step is **reporting the compensation for the work done** via the permanent establishment with consideration of the arm's length principle. Referred to along with this are:

- the functions of the company carried out via the permanent establishment or another part of the company,
- assets used, and
- risks assumed.

Question 238

What results from documentation are being omitted?

Answer

If no separate accounting records are prepared for the permanent establishment, profits attributable to the permanent establishment could be determined through the **indirect method**, i.e. the overall profit of the enterprise will be allocated to the permanent establishment according to a certain distribution basis. This method is applicable if it is common in the country where the permanent establishment lies. Generally speaking, however, this method should only be used as an **exception to the rule**. 26

If the taxpayer does not comply with his/her obligation to file, it is a regulatory offence that is punishable by fine. If it comes to be seen as a case of frivolous tax evasion, there can be a fine of up to 50,000 € imposed. If there are no documents provided, a **penalty payment** can be set and the basis for taxation is estimated by the German tax authorities. 27

Question 239

What happens from a tax perspective if the employee leaves Germany or quits?

Answer

If the employee leaves Germany or quits, the conditions for the existence of a permanent representative are considered gone as well, as is the existence of the company's representative permanent establishment. As with the opening of a permanent establishment in Germany, the closing of one **must be communicated** to the German tax authorities. 28

Chapter 20 Posting of Employees/Business Trips | Entsendungen/Dienstreisen

Definition, Legal Principles
Due to the constantly increasing international integration of markets and the corresponding competitive pressures that come with them, many companies have come to recognize the necessity of sending their employees on foreign assignments. In connection with foreign assignment of employees, **different terminology** is used, usually dependent on the assignment's length.

A foreign assignment can take form by posting employees, business trip(s), cross-border commercial employee leasing or temporary employment abroad. Being posted is often an **indispensable step to climb the carrier ladder**, especially in businesses that work internationally. By taking on such an assignment, the employee shows the employer the flexibility, competence and ability to cope with other general conditions such as different languages, cultures or unfamiliar economic systems. Further still, posting an employee abroad be the basis of economic opportunities. Often the transfer or posting of employees is about building up overseas production and transferring employee knowledge and expertise abroad.

Question 240
Is an employee required to work abroad?

Answer
1 Yes, if the employment contract includes it.

Question 241
When is a stay abroad referred to as business trip?

Answer
2 There is no uniform definition for the term business trip ("Dienstreise"). The German Federal Labor Court defines a business trip to be a trip to a place outside of the regular work site where official business is to be carried out. This definition requires that the employee performs a **work-related task** at the other place. With a business trip, one refers to a stay of **no more than three months**, be it domestic or abroad. Note that business trips have no affect on an employment contract. Moreover, such a trip does not effect change of tax liability if that trip is under 183 days per annum.

Question 242
Does the employee have to go on business trips?

Answer

Yes, even if the obligation to take business trips is seldom found in employment contracts. This obligation does not require explicit or individual agreement. The business trip has to have a **connection to the work the employee does** for the employer and the employer has to authorize the power to give directives. Employees who are out sick may not be sent on business trips. The employer also has to take into consideration severe disabilities the employee may have. 3

Question 243

What does one refer to with a temporary posting of employees?

Answer

A posting of employees is based on the employee's existing employment contract, and the employee is to be working for the German employer abroad or one of its foreign subsidiaries due to a **special contractual agreement** based on instruction the employer has given the employee. 4

Question 244

Does the posting of employees require a work permit in Germany?

Answer

Yes. The German Federal Employment Agency is responsible for that. 5

Question 245

What is an employee assignment agreement ("Entsendungsvertrag")?

Answer

An employee assignment agreement is the legal basis for temporarily assigning (posting) an employee to work abroad. There are **different contract models** that should be determined by the particular situation and depend on the length and type of the employment abroad. In other words, the choice of a suitable contract is contingent on the length of stay, the work to be carried out as well as the position and situation in which the posting of the employee takes place. 6

Question 246

Can an employee be transferred to a location abroad?

Answer

7 Yes, if the prerequisites for posting of employees are met or if the employee is going to be located abroad. For this purpose, the German employment contract can be suspended and the employee can conclude a **temporary employment contract with the foreign company**.

Question 247

Does the German employment contract end with the employee being posted elsewhere?

Answer

8 No, the allocation of the employee to the German company **remains intact** despite the assignment being a foreign posting. In addition to the existing German employment contract, however, an assignment agreement would be made.

Question 248

When does a foreign assignment mean the German employment agreement ends?

Answer

9 The German employment contract ends when the employee quits or is dismissed.

Question 249

What applies in cases of transfers?

Answer

10 The German employment contract is suspended for transfers and is replaced by a supplemental, fixed-term foreign assignment agreement. Added to this is a fixed-term employment contract with the foreign partner (or subsidiary) company. This agreement is in effect for the duration of the foreign assignment stay. An employee is **only loosely connected with the employer located in Germany** during this assignment. In addition, the employee has a contract with the foreign (subsidiary) company. The employee would still be taken care of by the German personnel department and reports occasionally to the corporate headquarters.

Question 250

When does the German Employee Posting Act ("Arbeitnehmerentsendegesetz – AEntG") take effect?

Answer

The German Employee Posting Act has **mandatory application** between an employer with headquarters abroad and his/her employee within the scope of a collective bargaining agreement. One requirement is that the business or business unit is operating in the **spirit of the framework of the collective bargaining agreement** for the given industry. The domestic employer has to allow at least for the working conditions applicable to and afforded under the collective bargaining agreement in the given industry. The German Employee Posting Act further offers a **legal framework** for setting the minimum wage in a collective bargaining agreement for a given sector binding, regardless of whether the employer is headquartered domestically or abroad. 11

Question 251

Is the posting of employees permissible in every industry?

Answer

No, the industries where this is allowed include: 12
- construction,
- commercial cleaning,
- letter delivery,
- laundry and security services,
- specialized mining work,
- waste management, and
- educational and training services.

Question 252

What does someone in Germany speak of when referring to the commercial leasing of employees?

Answer

The leasing of employees, also referred to as **contract staffing**, finds its legal basis in the German Temporary Employment Act ("Arbeitnehmerüberlassungsgesetz – AÜG"). According to the provisions of this act, the leasing of employees occurs if the employer (lender) allocates an employee to a third party (borrower) on the basis of an employee leasing agreement. With this arrangement, the lent employee remains in an **employment relationship with the lender** during the time that he/she is completely integrated into the borrower's organization, in order to work for the promotion of the company in accordance with the ideas and aims of the borrower and its employees. During the lending out period, the leased out employee is subject to the **borrower's right to instruct** his/her employees ("Weisungsrecht"). 13

Question 253

Is an employee required to work abroad for a third party at the request of the employer in case of commercial leasing?

Answer

14 Yes, if conditions for the commercial leasing of the employee exist. In addition, the German employer has to conclude a **service or work contract** with the third party that comport with German norms.

Question 254

Does the employer require a permit or other authorization in order to assign an employee to work for a third party?

Answer

15 Yes, as professional commercial leasing of employees can only be carried out with the **permission of the German Employment Agency**. And, this applies not only to all occasional, sufficiently independent work, but also to that which is long-term and has the intention of economic benefit. Only rarely are exceptions made.

Question 255

Do employers need permission for reassignments within their organization?

Answer

16 No, as the work assignment has to be between an affiliated company when it is irrelevant whether the employee is leased to or borrowed from the dependent company. The commercial leasing of employees **can only be temporary**. What is significant is whether, according to underlying provisions, the employee should return to his original company or he/she leaves the firm for good.

Chapter 21 Pregnancy/Parental Leave | Schwangerschaft/Elternzeit

Definition, Legal Principles

!

In 2011, approximately 663,000 children were born in Germany, with a large number of mothers working in addition to fathers. The spirit of German laws on the matter hold that the employment relationship of pregnant woman and their unborn children should be **protected from workplace dangers** during the pregnancy by the provisions of extant maternity laws. Further, legal principles are the prescription of occupational health and safety regulations for the protection of mothers ("Mutterschutzarbeitsplatzverordnung – MuSchArbV"). Generally, these protections apply to all pregnant women, even those in minijobs, working out of the home, or in trainee- or apprenticeships. There is also the possibility of taking **parental leave after the birth** of the child, the longest period being through the end of the child's third year of life. By way of parental leave, parents should be given the chance to dedicate their time to raising and caring for their child without the fear of their employment relationship being terminated by their respective employer.

I. General Aspects

Question 256

What is the difference between pregnancy leave and parental leave?

Answer

Pregnancy describes, of course, the period during which a mother carries a baby to term. However, parental leave begins with the birth of the child. 1

Parental leave has the purpose of **making the care for and rearing of a child easier** for working parents and guardians. During the term of the parental leave, the employer releases the employee from having to perform the work the employee does. 2

Expecting mothers can choose whether or not to work during the **six weeks leading up to the birth** of their child. However, mothers are **strictly prohibited** from working in the **eight weeks after their baby's birth**. This is a right mothers cannot waive. 3

II. Pregnancy

Question 257

Are there prohibitions on working and under what conditions?

Answer

Expecting mothers may not work in the six weeks prior to their child's birth unless she **clearly states her intent to work**. Beyond this, expecting mothers may not 4

work if the job being performed has **detrimental effects**, e.g. radiation or substances that could harm her health or subject her to harmful vapors of gases. Further, expecting mothers may not perform:
- extra work/overtime,
- night shifts,
- work on weekends or holidays.

5 Lastly, mothers are **strictly prohibited** from working in the first eight weeks after their baby's birth.

Question 258
From what point in time can a mother return to work?

Answer
6 A mother may not work until eight weeks postpartum.[1] During the **eight-week period postpartum**, mothers are strictly prohibited from working in Germany. In individual cases where a woman either gives birth to multiple children or prematurely delivers a child, the period of legal protection is **extended to twelve weeks after delivery** of the child or children. In order for a premature birth to be medically determined to be as such, a medical certificate testifying to this fact is required. Should the child weigh under 2,500 grams or the child if he/she has not reached the necessary signs of maturity set by qualified medical professionals, the child is considered by German law to be premature. If the child was born exceptionally early, the legal protection may be extended even further and would be increased by the precise amount of time the baby was born early.

Question 259
Can a pregnant woman be dismissed from her job?

Answer
7 No, a pregnant woman may not be dismissed from her job for **up to four months postpartum**. That said, her employer has to know about the pregnancy, or be made aware no later than two weeks following receipt of her termination notice.

1 See also Chapter 21 margin number 6.

III. Motherhood Allowance

Question 260
What is the so-called motherhood allowance ("Mutterschaftsgeld")?

Answer
Motherhood allowance is a **subsidy**. It is paid during the phase when the mother is 8
under maternity protection. In Germany, that means six weeks prior to and eight weeks after birth of the child.

Question 261
Does an entitlement to motherhood allowance exist?

Answer
An entitlement exists only if the woman has a fixed employment relationship with 9
the employer. This also includes women who are working out of the home. Additionally, the woman has to have **statutory health care coverage**. Otherwise, when she is insured privately, the woman receives a one-time motherhood allowance payment.

IV. Parental Leave

Question 262
Who is entitled to parental leave?

Answer
Employees who are entitled to parental leave include those, be they male or female, 10
who have a **working relationship with the given employer at the time of applying** for this leave, and this includes those employees completing vocational training, part-time employees, temporary employees, students doing side jobs and those working from home and those in equivalent employment relationships. Others who have a right to parental leave are adoptive parents, foster parents, or relatives of the child. The former have rights similar to the biological parents; the latter have these rights only in special cases.

Question 263
Can someone be barred from his/her right to parental leave entitlement?

Answer

11 No, the entitlement to parental leave is **mandatory statutory law**. It cannot be barred by contract or limited.

12 Work agreements and collective bargaining agreements that affect the employment status of the employee before or after the parental leave are **illegal.** With the presentation of qualifying criteria for the entitlement, the **employer cannot legally prevent an employee from taking parental leave**.

Question 264

Are there special rules regarding adopted and foster children?

Answer

13 Yes, parental leave can be taken for adopted and foster children for a **three-year period** beginning at the time the child is officially taken into the employee's home. It ends once the child reaches his/her eighth birthday.

Question 265

Does there need to be a written contract about parental leave?

Answer

14 An explanation of the usage is required. Regarding content, German law requires that the employee requests parental leave and, at the same time, communicates the **specific dates** for the beginning and end of the time to be taken, taking the parental leave within two years. The employee has to request parental leave in writing and the employer has to certify it.

Question 266

What happens to the employment relationship with the employer during parental leave?

Answer

15 The employment relationship continues, but the **primary job obligations are suspended** for the duration of the parental leave.

Question 267

Can someone on parental leave be dismissed from a job?

Answer

In Germany, there is a **special protection** against unfair dismissal. This special protection is valid from the point in time when parental leave that is in line with procedures and deadlines is requested. The protection exists during the parental leave and no more than eight weeks before the start of that leave. During the time special protection against unfair dismissal is valid, the employer may not terminate the employment relationship he/she has with the employee. Only in **exceptional cases** can the highest state-level office responsible for employment protection matters or a authority it has designated declare such a termination permissible. 16

Question 268

May the employer mandate parental leave?

Answer

No, the claim to parental leave **depends entirely on the initiative of the employee**. So, if the employee does not request parental leave, the employer cannot, for example, thereby counteract an existing overstaffing issue by way of his/her authority to give directions in a given situation. 17

Question 269

Are there particular deadlines to observe?

Answer

Yes, the notification period to make the claim is usually **seven weeks**. A shorter time limit is only possible if urgent reasons prevent adherence to the standard period. 18

Question 270

For how long can someone go on parental leave?

Answer

According to German law, an employee may take parental leave **until the child's third birthday**. The time of the maternity protection period is to be deducted from that, which is counted against the time allotted. Parental leave ends with the end of the child's third year of life. In other words, the employee has to return to work by the child's third birthday. So long as the employer agrees, up to a **twelve-month portion** of parental leave can be taken at a later time, and that time must be before the **child's eighth birthday**. 19

Question 271
How much parental leave is there if there are fewer than three years between the birth of other children?

Answer
20 In cases of multiple children, parents are entitled to **three years of parental leave for each child**, even if the three-year-time limit alluded to in the German Law on Parental Allowance and Parental Leave ("Gesetz zum Elterngeld und zur Elternzeit – BEEG") has been exceeded.

Question 272
Can parental leave be broken up into different time periods?

Answer
21 Yes, parental leave can be **split into two time periods**; breaking the leave down into more time periods requires the agreement of the employer.

Question 273
Can parental leave be extended?

Answer
22 The initially intended time period can be extended by mutual agreement. Thus, the consent of the employer is required. The employer therefore possesses the **right to reject** an extension of parental leave until it verges on abuse of the right and may be construed as harassment.

Question 274
Can parental leave be ended early?

Answer
23 Shortening the declared time of parental leave is only permissible with the **consent of the employer**. Otherwise the ability of the employer to rely on his business planning is endangered. Thus, the consent is at the discretion of the employer. Other rules apply in more difficult situations, such as cases of a child's premature death.

Question 275
Does illness prior to the planned start of parental leave have an effect on the ability to take the leave?

Answer

No, as the parties involved will have already made a binding agreement. The same 24
applies when the parental leave ends. Even if the employee is ill to this point, parental leave ends as agreed upon.

Question 276

Are parents on parental leave entitled to vacation time?

Answer

Yes, but not in its entirety. Employers are entitled to reduce the vacation time the 25
employee has for a given year by **one-twelfth for each month** of the parental leave. However, if the employee works part-time during the parental leave, the employer does not have a right to reduce the employee's vacation time.

Question 277

May an employee work elsewhere during parental leave?

Answer

Yes, but the employee needs the employer's consent in order take on another em- 26
ployment. To this end, there **must be an application made** in which the specific type and amount of time for the alternative work is communicated to the employer. Furthermore, the other employer has to be named in the application.

V. Parental-leave Allowance

Question 278

What is parental-leave allowance ("Elterngeld")?

Answer

Parental-leave allowance is a **governmental social benefit** and subsidy for fami- 27
lies.

Question 279

Who is entitled to the parental-leave allowance?

Answer

A **cut-off date regulation** applies with respect to the parental-leave allowance. That 28
means that parents whose child was born on or after January 1, 2007 receive the

benefit. The parent entitled to an income replacement benefit is the one who stops working after the child's birth in order to care for the child.

Question 280
How much can the parental-leave allowance be?

Answer
29 Mothers or fathers will receive monthly payments of **67% of their last net income** (on average, twelve months before the child's birth); the cap is 1,800 € per month.

Question 281
How long is parental-leave allowance paid out?

Answer
30 Parental-leave allowance is **limited to twelve months**. It can, however, be extended to 14 months if both partners stop working. The so-called "partner months" can be freely divided during those two extra months.

Question 282
Who can apply for parental-leave allowance?

Answer
31 Parental-leave allowance has to be applied for at the office responsible for education allowances ("Erziehungsgeldstelle"); depending on where you live in Germany, it is either the youth or social welfare office.

VI. Part-time Work during Parental Leave

Question 283
Does the employer have to offer a part-time position to parents who are taking parental leave?

Answer
32 The German Law on Parental Allowance and Parental Leave provides for the possibility of working part-time during parental leave. Accordingly, employees – male or female – are entitled to working part-time **for the duration of their parental leave.** However, the right to part-time work in accordance with the German Law on Parental Allowance and Parental Leave is different than the one under the Act on Part-

Time and Fixed-Term Employment ("Teilzeitvorschriften des Teilzeit- und Befristungsgesetzes – TzBfG"). One **considerable difference** between Part-time Work and Fixed-term Employment Contracts Act and the Parental Allowance and Parental Leave rights to working part-time is that the **latter right is only protected for the duration of the parental leave**. However, the part-time work entitlement according to the Part-time Work and Fixed-term Employment Contracts Act changes the scope of contractually required working time for perpetuity. At the end of the parental leave, the employee is again contractually obliged to work without a need for an explicit agreement by the contracting parties.

Question 284
What information needs to be in the application to work part-time?

Answer
An application for part-time work during parental leave has to lay out the **start and** 33
scope of the shortened work day. The employee can give the desired break down of the shortened work day.

Chapter 22 Probationary Work | Probezeit

! **Definition, Legal Principles**

Taking on new employees represents a long-term investment for the employer. In this context employers are interested in testing new employees before establishing a long-term employment relationship with the employee and can then only dissolve that relationship with him/her with lengthy notification periods that comport with the German Employment Protection Act ("Kündigungsschutzgesetz – KSchG"). This has the particular purpose of **testing the capabilities** and their respectful and polite manner of dealing with co-workers. If the evaluation turns out to be negative, the employer can let that employee go in relatively short order. The shortened notification period in such a case would be two weeks. Beyond this, the employer is entitled to fire that employee **without providing grounds** for doing so. In practice permanent employment agreements with introductory probationary periods are the most common form of work trials. There are additionally **short-term employment relationships** that are on a trail basis and end at the conclusion of the probationary period and continue with a permanent contract with the successful completion of the probationary period.

Question 285

How long is a standard probationary period in Germany? Does the amount of time differ for traineeships and regular jobs?

Answer

1 German law sets a limit on probationary periods only for traineeships or apprenticeships. In such cases, probationary periods **may not exceed four months.** In practice, probationary periods last **six months**, so long as a different time frame is not stipulated in a collective bargaining agreement. In fact probationary periods should not exceed six months. One lasting longer generally would be seen as not making much sense in Germany, because the German Employment Protection Act ("Kündigungsschutzgesetz") is not mandatorily applicable for companies of over ten employees after six months, so a simplified notice of termination in the probationary period is no longer possible.

Question 286

How long is the period of notice during the probationary period?

Answer

2 According to law a **notice period of two weeks** is the norm, so long as a collective bargaining agreement does not set forth a different time frame. Notice of termination can be given on any day of the week. A two-week notice period can even be given on the last day of probationary period.

Question 287
Can a probationary period be extended?

Answer
Generally, yes. However, it is nevertheless uncommon. The reduced notice period during the probationary period cannot be extended beyond a six-month period. Moreover, the **general protection against unfair dismissal** comes into play after the existence of a six-month long employment relationship in companies with more than ten employees, agreement on a longer probationary period notwithstanding. 3

Question 288
What alternatives are there?

Answer
It is possible to declare a longer notification period or include the matter of termination in a side letter, one that advises on the conclusion of a new employment relationship if the employee has proven the existence of one. Such an agreement can also be agreed to in a **severance agreement**. 4

Question 289
Are there rights to vacation time during the probationary period?

Answer
The employee generally has a right to **1/12th of his annual vacation time each month**, even during the probationary period. However, the employer can impose a ban on taking leave during the probationary period, which means that the employee has to forego completely his/her vacation time. The right to vacation time is then taken **after successful completion** of the probationary period. If the employee is let go during the probationary period, the employer has to **remunerate that employee for the unused vacation time**. On the other hand, if the employee has used too much vacation time during the probationary period, the employer cannot request that money back from the employee. 5

Question 290
What happens if the employee is unable to work (e.g. due to illness) during the probationary period?

Answer

6 If the employee is unable to work during the probationary period due to a longer-standing illness, the sense and intent of the probationary period – the testing of the employee – cannot be achieved. Nevertheless, the employee's probationary period is **not automatically extended** for the time he/she had been absent. It does not represent a net period of probationary employment. Contrarily, there is nothing preventing the parties from mutually agreeing to an extension of the probationary period.

Chapter 23 Professional Schooling/Training | Ausbildung

Definition, Legal Principles
Professional schooling/training in Germany has a **dual structure.** It is mostly carried out in the initial vocational training of youth, which takes place at two locations – the company and in a vocational school. The vocational training at the company is regulated by German national law, the Vocational Training Act ("Berufsbildungsgesetz – BBiG"). It is there, in the companies themselves, where the practical portion of the vocational training is taught to the trainees. The theoretical portion of the schooling is covered by the vocational schools. There is **principally no age limit** for one to begin his/her traineeship.

In 2010, there were approximately 1.5 million trainees in Germany. There were 551,272 on-the-job training agreements signed in 2012. At the same time there were a record number of vacant traineeship posts in Germany, 33,275 of them.

Question 291
How does professional schooling/training work in Germany?

Answer
Company schooling/training takes place in a so-called **dual system.** This system 1
includes the concurrent schooling at a trade school and at a company that takes on trainees. The trainees attend work-related course instruction in a trade school along side of practical training at an actual place of business. As a rule the schooling portion is **no more than two days per week** or takes place in multiple teaching blocks per year. In most instances the duration of the hands-on training amounts to **three or three-and-one-half years,** but it can also be reduced to two years for exceptional performance or for special educational background (e.g. "Abitur", the secondary qualification diploma needed for university admittance). Those seeking a training slot at a company apply directly to the company taking on trainees.

Question 292
Who covers the training costs?

Answer
The main portion of the training costs is **covered by the company** taking on train- 2
ees; only a small portion of the cost is covered by the trainee.

Question 293
Does the trainee need to be hired?

Answer

3 Generally not. However, slightly different rules may apply in a collective bargaining agreement. Moreover, **different rules can apply** if a member of the young workers and trainees submits an application for hire in a timely fashion. Then the company has to hire and offer a position to the trainee.

Question 294

Is the hiring/firing process the same for trainees as it is for other employees?

Answer

4 As a rule, trainees in Germany will be used as **regular employees.** According to sec. 10, para. 2 of the Vocational Training Act, only legislation dealing with employment contracts in force applies, so long as the Vocational Training Act does not offer other rights or protections. Differences to the employment contract appear, on the hand, during the **probationary period**. This has to be at least one month and no longer than four months during the practical part of the vocational schooling. Vocational training relationships have set durations. They end when the schooling does. Termination of employment during the probationary period at any time without compliance with a notice period is possible. The vocational training can only be terminated after the probationary period only with a good reason or if the trainee quits. In this sense the trainee enjoys a **special protection from termination**. If the trainee wishes to defend him/herself from termination, he/she needs to appeal to an arbitration board in most instances.

Question 295

What is "Duales Studium" understood to mean?

Answer

5 In this dual system of vocational education and academic studies, students enter into a sort of on-the-job training agreement with a company. It is basically the same as **cooperative education programs** found in the United States. Such programs differentiate themselves from traditional college studies above all else through the significantly high amount of practical training involved. In Germany, the student contracts him/herself to work for the company when not taking classes. In return the student receives what is ultimately a **scholarship** for the time of study, which is a considerable financial reward for the student. Rules about taking the student on as an employee at the conclusion of studies are also in part negotiated, so that the student is obligated to work for the company for a set period of time. This establishes a **reciprocal relationship between the trainee and company**.

Question 296

Does a person's age play a role in his/her being a trainee?

Answer

The German Youth Employment Protection Act ("Jugendarbeitsschutzgesetz – 6
JArbSchG") applies here for trainees who are minors. According to it, youth have, among other things, an entitlement to **more paid vacation and special working time regulations**.

Question 297

Are trainees entitled to the same amount of vacation and sick leave?

Answer

Yes, regulations on vacation time and continued remuneration apply for employee 7
as well as working trainees. Like every employee, every trainee has a **right to vacation time**. The Continued Payment of Wages and Salaries Act ("Entgeltfortzahlungsgesetz") understands an employee in this context as including those employees who are still in the training phase of their employment.

Chapter 24 Protective Rights | Schutzrechte

Definition, Legal Principles
A number of policies that protect employees exist in Germany. Legal regulations that protect workers include unfair dismissal protection, working time protections, vacation time guaranties and continued remuneration (for example, when one is on vacation). Along with material employer protection policies, technical occupational health and safety is also guaranteed by way of policies on employee safety (safety of workplace, production plants, machines and tools as well as other working materials). In this way the protection of employees' health and safety is purposefully achieved.

Beyond this **particular groups of employers enjoy special protections** by way of special regulations, since some employees are dependent on the company due to particular life situations and are thus especially worthy of legal protection. Some examples of such groups include expecting mothers, trainees, teens and the severely handicapped.

Question 298
What protective rights are there for pregnant women?

Answer
1 According to German law, employers may not terminate their employment relationship with pregnant women for the entire term of the pregnancy or the four months following the child's birth. Additionally, expecting mothers may not work in the **six weeks prior to their child's birth** unless they clearly state their intent to work. Beyond this, expecting mothers may not work if the job being performed has **detrimental effects** to their health. Expecting mothers may not perform:
- extra work/overtime,
- night shifts,
- work on weekends or holidays.

Question 299
What are the protective laws in place for mothers?

Answer
2 Mothers may not work for up to the conclusion of an **eight-week period after their child's birth**; in cases of premature and multiple births, that time is extended up to twelve weeks.

Question 300
What are the protective laws in place for minors?

Answer

Under German law, minors enjoy special legal protection. They cannot be contractually bound before the end of their seventh year of life. Minors that have reached the age of seven are **entitled to limited rights**. That means that they can conclude a valid contract if their parents, guardian or legally recognized proxy consents to the agreement. With a view to **liability**, torts law provides for protection of minors against liability. Accordingly, minors under age seven are not liable for their negotiations unless liability is provided under special circumstances. Up until they reach legal age, minors are only liable insofar as they can recognize their injustice. 3

Question 301

What needs to be kept in mind when employing severely handicapped persons?

Answer

The severely handicapped are entitled to **preferential treatment** from their employer with respect to in-house measures and to handicap-accessible facilities and furnishings in the workplace. Severely handicapped persons also enjoy **special protection against unfair dismissal**. Employers have to obtain the consent of the German Office for Equal Employment Opportunity ("Integrationsamt") before terminating a severely handicapped person. 4

Question 302

What kind of job security does the employer have to guaranty?

Answer

Employers have to guaranty **occupational safety and security**. They have to protect employees from dangers that are typical or even atypical to that business sector. They are further obligated to take all possible steps to ensure health in the workplace. The three-steps of occupational safety employers have to guaranty are as follows: 5

- determination of hazards,
- duty to report, and
- duty to take action on them.

Question 303

How do employers have to determine what hazards for employers exist at the given company's premises?

Answer

6 The hazards have to be identified and documented. The protective measures already taken have to be continuously tested and adapted to changing stipulations. Employers also have to **give all required information** to employees and inform them about on-site hazards (e.g. poor fixtures, furniture, inadequate ventilation, etc.) they may be confronted with. Finally, employers have to **implement necessary protective measures without delay**. They have to obey **accident prevention measures**, which means, for example, observing and implementing the Ordinance on Placement of Visual Display Units (PC monitors).

Question 304

What are the health and safety regulations for youth?

Answer

7 German law states that teenagers under the age of 15 may not conclude a contract. However, there are **exceptions for internships and vacation jobs**. Teenagers may not work more than eight hours per day and no more than 40 hours per week. Employers have to release teenagers to participate in vocational school instruction. Other than that, the German Youth Employment Protection Act ("Jugendarbeitsschutzgesetz") protects teens with respect to

- sufficient breaks,
- shift times,
- daily free-time,
- being permitted to sleep at night,
- being off on Saturdays, Sundays, and holidays,
- vacation and dangerous work (e.g. work that involves accident hazards).

8 That said, teens may work on weekends in certain industries. Some examples include homes for the elderly, entertainment industry (e.g. DJs, selling movie tickets, filming weddings) and automobile garages. The teen working on weekends nevertheless must have at least two Saturdays off per month. Similar rules apply for Sundays.

Question 305

Does the employer have to guaranty medical service(s)?

Answer

9 Yes, the employer has to appoint a company physician and trained personnel for occupational safety that support safety at work and with accident prevention. The employer may only appoint people as company doctors who are **licensed to practice medicine**.

Company physicians are to be brought in when their services are necessary at the company. According to section 5 of the Occupational Safety Act ("Arbeitssicherheitsgesetz"), the following points are of considerable importance for bringing a physician: 10

- the type of business,
- the accident and health risks for employees there,
- the number of employees and,
- the company organization.

Chapter 25 Reduced Working Hours (Short-time) | Kurzarbeit

Definition, Legal Principles

In times of **harsh international economic and financial crisis**, reduced working times represent an important means of securing jobs. It therefore makes sense that, from 2008, the number of those working in "short-time" positions steadily increased for quite some time. In May 2009, the number of short-time workers peaked at 1.4 million. Afterward, that number gradually sank. By October 2012, the level had come down to 72,000 workers.[1]

The sense and purpose of this special form of employment is to correct what is most often a **temporary imbalance** due to increase in workload needs and working employees without having to issue termination notices. It boils down to setting aside working hours and a simultaneously reducing compensation accordingly. The requirement for situations that call for a reduction in working hours is regulated by the German Social Security Code, Book III ("SGB III").

Question 306

What is understood by reduced working hours ("Kurzarbeit") in Germany?

Answer

1 Sometimes referred to as "short-time" in English, the German concept of "Kurzarbeit" is an instrument of labor market policy. Financed by **unemployment insurance contributions**, it serves to reduce working hours and avoid layoffs. With it there is a temporary decrease independent of the regular legal requirements, which can develop differently depending on the crisis at hand. The practice customarily accomplished by businesses and set out in employment contracts with regard to a reduction in working hours is a correspondingly **simultaneous reduction in pay** which is subsidized by the German Employment Agency.

Question 307

What might lead to reduced working hours in Germany?

Answer

2 Reduced working hours can be the result of **economic reasons** such as the financial or banking crisis 2008/2009, **seasonal reasons** (e.g. seasonal allowance for reduced

1 German Federal Employment Agency Statistics, The Job Market in Germany ("Der Arbeitsmarkt in Deutschland") – Cyclical Short-time Work ("Konjunkturelle Kurzarbeit"), date of reference: January 2013 (http://statistik.arbeitsagentur.de/Statischer-Content/Arbeitsmarktberichte/Berichte-Broschueren/Arbeitsmarkt/Generische-Publikationen/Kug-Bericht-2013-01.pdf).

working hours, or "Saison-Kurzarbeitergeld") and in cases of commercial, long-term **restructuring measures** (allowance for reduced working hours during business restructuring, or "Transfer-Kurzarbeitergeld").

Question 308
What advantages exist for the employer with "Kurzarbeit"?

Answer
Advantages are: 3
- a temporary lowering of personnel costs during economically hard times for the company,
- the safeguarding of company liquidity,
- compensation for loss of wages and stabilization of jobs,
- job preservation,
- avoidance of having to hand out pink slips (official German term: "Beendigungskündigungen") and dismissal disputes,
- prevention against long-term unemployment,
- receipt of employee specialized skill (training),
- increase in the flexibility with respect to company's employment policies,
- competitive advantage by gaining more employee know-how in an economic upturn,
- temporary take-over of the operational and economic risks by the German Federal Employment Agency.

Question 309
What disadvantages do reduced working hours present to the employer?

Answer
Disadvantages are: 4
- time needed for coordinating with the appropriate employment agency,
- time spent on requests, administrative costs, complex calculation and payment of the reduced working hours allowances,
- applying to the German Federal Employment Agency for the reimbursement of paid out reduced-working-hours allowances,
- premature stopping of the agreed upon reduced working hours,
- voluntary resignation of employees and the loss of know-how.

Question 310
Who can apply for reduced working hours?

Answer

5 German companies and operational divisions of them with **at least one employee** can apply for reduced working hours and the corresponding allowance, though the German Employment Promotion Act ("Arbeitsförderungsrecht") of the German Social Security Code III ("Sozialgesetzbuch III – SGB III") refers to the domestic job market.

Question 311

How can an employer introduce reduced working times in Germany?

Answer

6 An employer has to provide a **written notice** to the German Federal Employment Agency office located near the company or operational division. This notice has to make a **convincing case** for the considerable loss of work hours and the operational requirements for the reduced working time allowance. The German Federal Employment Agency has blank forms to complete for this purpose. The German Federal Employment Agency has to promptly provide a written response to the conditions provided in the notice.

Question 312

Are reduced working hours ("Kurzarbeit") state subsidized?

Answer

7 Yes, the German government subsidizes "Kurzarbeit".

Question 313

Where does the application for the reduced working hour allowance need to be sent?

Answer

8 The application for the reduced working time allowance is to be sent to the German Federal Employment Agency office in the region where the company or its payroll office is located.

Question 314

Who has the right to apply?

Answer

9 **Companies** have the right to apply, not employees who may prospectively receive benefits.

Question 315

Does the works council need to agree?

Answer

Yes, German law grants the works council **co-determination rights**, thus it partici- 10
pates in such decisions.

Chapter 26 Reference (from Employers) | Zeugnis

Definition, Legal Principles

In Germany employees have a right to a written reference at the end of the employment relationship. The legal basis may be found in sec. 109 of the German Industrial Code ("Gewerbeordnung – GewO"), which **applies uniformly to all employees** in Germany.

For trainees and apprentices, the right to a reference is controlled by the German Vocational Act ("Bundesbildungsgesetz – BBiG"). Above all, an employee reference serves the employee's further professional development. The reference enables the employee to prove his/her **job history** and **personal and professional capabilities**. Additionally, the reference helps future employers in the process of selecting new employees.

On the one hand, the reference must conform to the truth; on the other hand, it should reflect the good will of the employer. Due to the tension between good will and obligation to tell the truth, it is not uncommon that disputes over the contents of references come before labor courts. The reason may be the well-known **"secret code" of references**: what seems to be a positively worded characteristic can have a certain touch or hint that can lead one to draw a negative conclusion. In exceptional, justifiable cases (e.g. change in supervisor) an **interim performance review** is also justified.

Question 316

Is every employee entitled to an employer reference letter?

Answer

1 Yes, in Germany every employee has a **right to a reference** from his/her employer.

Question 317

What function does this reference serve?

Answer

2 The reference serves the **professional advancement** of the employee. It also gives employers who are looking for staff-selection criteria for filling positions.

Question 318

When does the reference have to be issued by the employer?

Answer

3 The employer owes the employee the reference **at the end of the employment relationship.** A general letter of reference has to be produced without the urging of the employee. A "qualifiziertes Zeugnis" – a reference detailing the qualifications of the employee (e.g. supervisory roles, accomplishments, etc.) – is to be issued if the employee expresses that he/she needs one.

Question 319
What is in a basic reference ("einfaches Zeugnis")?

Answer
The type of work and length of time worked by the employee are to be denoted. 4

Question 320
What is in a "qualifiziertes Zeugnis"?

Answer
As suggested earlier, the term "qualified" is not negatively applied here; a German 5
"qualified" reference from the employer has to include **all important facts** about and assessments of the employee that would be **of interest and significance to future employers**. For example, information about the performance and conduct of the employee are to be indicated. Note: The evaluation of job performance has to be based on the job description. The **employee's conduct** addresses the social behavior between him/her and superiors, co-workers and others in the workplace.

Question 321
What are "Bescheinigungen"?

Answer
As compared to the "Zeugnis", or reference from the employer, the "Bescheinigun- 6
gen" are certificates that represent **evidence of the nature of the employment with third parties**. In Germany, a "Zeugnis" is generally understood to mean one which is "qualified", one that indicates the accomplishments and positive aspects of the employee's person and work. The common understanding of "einfaches Zeugnis" is that of a mere certificate indicating employment.

Question 322
What is the general content needed for a reference from the given employer?

Answer
The content is determined by how the purpose of supporting the employee's profes- 7
sional advancement can best be served. That means the appearance, choice of words, date created and who signs it have to **correspond with the normal customs** of business operations.

Question 323
How should a typical German reference from an employer look (e.g. handwritten, what paper, etc.)?

Answer
8 A reference should be typed and **on the company letterhead** that is used in regular business; on that paper the full address and company name, legal form (e.g. Inc., GmbH, etc.) and the current address are to be listed.

Question 324
What employee HR information has to be included in the reference from the employer?

Answer
9 The precise and full first and last name of the employee, and, where appropriate, date of birth are to be indicated. The date of birth is only to be included **with employee consent**.

Question 325
Does a reference from the employer have to show the reference's issue date?

Answer
10 Yes, and the reference's issue date and the date of its actual creation are **usually the same**.

Question 326
By whom does the reference from the employer have to be signed?

Answer
11 A reference from the employer is finalized when **signed by the employer by hand** or its negotiating representative. Facsimiles, photocopied signatures, e-mails or faxes are insufficient.

Question 327
Does the reference from the employer have to include employee health information?

Answer
12 No, employee health information does not belong in a reference from the employer.

Question 328

Does the employee's membership in the works council or trade union involvement have to be included?

Answer

No, that would only be included **at the request** of the employee. 13

Question 329

Is it common in Germany to include a grade for the employee in the reference from the employer?

Answer

Giving a grade to the employee is not required, but **it is common** to evaluate the 14
employee's work with a grade (they would be as follows: 1 = A; 1- = A-; 2+ = B+; 2 = B; 2- = B-, etc.).

Question 330

Does the reference from the employer have to include the reason why the employee is leaving?

Answer

Only **if the employee wishes** to have the reason for leaving included in the refer- 15
ence should it be included.

Question 331

Does the employer make him/herself liable for damages if he/she fails to provide the employee with a reference?

Answer

Yes, the employee could find the **employer culpable for damages** for a delayed 16
reference from that employer, if the letter is incorrect, or if the employer fails to even produce one. The damages due consists of the loss of income that the employee suffers by not getting the position applied for due to the current employer's delayed, incorrect or missing reference.

Chapter 27 Restructuring – Dismissal due to operational reasons | betriebsbedingte Kündigung

! **Definition, Legal Principles**

If operational requirements (e.g. volume of work diminishes) at a given company make plain that it **can no longer provide enough work** for one or more employees, the company has the possibility of announcing dismissals for operational reasons. But, the company can only do so if it comports with certain legal requirements. Some examples of operational circumstances that would allow for such dismissals in Germany include:

- restructuring,
- production cut-backs,
- sales and marketing difficulties or
- downsizing.

Thus, in Germany, dismissals due to operational reasons have to be justified by an urgent operational need, which also means that it has to be **impossible** for the company to place the employees affected in another job at the same company. In order to demonstrate the urgency of any dismissal for operational reasons, it is necessary to prove that the operational emergency cannot be addressed by a less burdensome method, e.g. a reduction of overtime or reduced working time(s). If an employee needs to be let go due to urgent operational needs, the employer may only do so when paying **consideration to relevant social factors** (e.g. number of dependents, age, etc.). More specifically, if one employee has young children and another is single with no children, both having a commensurable employment profile, the single employee with no children, the one who would in most instances be considered least vulnerable, is the one to be let go first in Germany. If such social considerations are not taken into consideration, dismissals for operational reasons are invalid.

Question 332

When can the employer lay off workers due to overstaffing?

Answer

1 An employer can dismiss workers due to overstaffing if the dismissal is necessary because of urgent operational needs that conflict with the continued employment of the given worker(s). It is essential that this be a business (as opposed to a personal) decision. More on that point, such a decision is only valid if it regards a **seriously meant business decision** and the implementation of organizational changes are at the company actually intended.

Question 333

What does it mean to decide based on social criteria ("Sozialauswahl")?

Answer

2 If an employer has to dismiss several employees, he/she has to ask the question: Which comparable employees can notice be given? But, employers are not freed of

responsibilities merely by making this decision. The employer also has to inform the employee dismissed about his/her **social fragility** ("soziale Schutzbedürftigkeit") when notice is given.

Question 334

How does selecting those to be dismissed based on social criteria work?

Answer

The employer has to sequence comparable employees in order to dismiss based 3
on social criteria. Selection based on social criteria is determined by **four attributes**:

- length of employment at the company,
- age,
- maintenance obligations (i.e. alimony, child support), and
- severe disabilities of the employee.

Question 335

What measures does the employer need to take action on before this?

Answer

Before a staff reduction, the employer is **obligated to take all possible counter-** 4
measures, such as reducing vacation time or arranging for overtime to be used or reducing working times.

Question 336

When does the Committee of Economic Policy have to be informed about the decision to restructure?

Answer

Employers have to inform the Committee on Economic Policy in a timely and com- 5
prehensive manner about the economic affairs of the company by presenting to them the information they require. The company is considered to have informed them **in a timely manner** if it does so before the company's decision has been made and consultation of the works council has taken place.

Question 337

When does the works council need to be informed in case of dismissal?

Answer

6 The law requires that the works council be **consulted on regarding every employee dismissal**. And, the employer has to provide the works council grounds for the dismissal(s). Further, notice about the dismissal(s) has to be provided before the actual dismissal. As there is no legally prescribed means of notification, the notification of dismissal(s) can be conveyed either in written form or orally.

Question 338

What rights does the works council have in this regard?

Answer

7 The right of the works council's participation in a hearing is enhanced by a **right to object**. The works council can object to an ordinary dismissal if the employer did not keep social concerns in mind or the dismissal violates a guideline of selection based on social criteria.

Question 339

What are the consequences of a works council objection?

Answer

8 The consequence of a works council objection is not that an ordinary dismissal has to be stopped, but that **substantive legal effects on the working relationship arise** which can help the affected employee in protection from unfair dismissal.

Question 340

What is "a balance of interests" ("Interessenausgleich")?

Answer

9 An "Interessenausgleich", the accommodating of conflicting interests, is a tool of employee participation in the spirit of the German Works Constitution Act. A subject of an "Interessenausgleich" is the question of **whether, when and how** the operational changes will be carried out. There should be an **agreement about the business decision** as such, e.g. at what point and in what way the company will be shut down, or, if applicable, how the personnel planning and employment of staff will happen and in what scope, and what form the operating procedure will take. Issues such as whether an employee is let to be go, transferred or retrained all fall under the umbrella of balancing interests.

Question 341

What is a “Sozialplan”?

Answer

A “Sozialplan” is a social plan regarding layoffs that is a balance of the economic 10
disadvantages that the employee encounters due to planned change in business and the avoidance thereof in the context of failed negotiations over a balancing of interests. The social plan has **compensatory and bridging function** as well as the **function of establishing peace**. It is concluded in accompaniment of the operational changes.

Question 342

What does the employer need to keep in mind if a large number of employees are going to be laid off (en masse layoffs – “Massenentlassung”)?

Answer

In cases of en masse layoffs, the employer has an obligation to **advertise and con-** 11
sult about the decision. The employer has to report the en masse layoff to the German Federal Employment Agency and the works council and share with the works council information about the layoff plans.[1]

---

1 See also Chapter 7.

Chapter 28 Retirement Plan | Altersversorgung

Definition, Legal Principles

Retirement plans define the entirety of all measures one takes in order to support one's self in old age. In Germany, retirement plans are **multifaceted** and are based on a **three-pillared system**, which consists of the state, company and private pension provisions.

The state old-age pension provision is a part of the German social security system, which acts as a retirement plan predominately for employees and their families. Regarding the **requirement to hold insurance**, contributions from employees are transferred to the corresponding health insurers. These insurers in turn apply the individual amounts to the respective German retirement insurance.

Monthly retirement payments are paid out to all who have reached the **age of 67** and were born in 1964 or later. For employees who were born prior to January 1, 1947, a retirement age of 65 applies. For those who were born between these times, there is a graduated scale regulating the time as which those individuals may retire (see chart[1] below).

Increase of the retirement age to 67

Year of birth of the insured person	Year of increase	Increase by months ...	... to the retirement age	
			Year	Month
1947	2013	1	65	1
1948	2013	2	65	2
1949	2014	3	65	3
1950	2015	4	65	4
1951	2016	5	65	5
1952	2017	6	65	6
1953	2018	7	65	7
1954	2019	8	65	8
1955	2020	9	65	9
1956	2021	10	65	10
1957	2022	11	65	11
1958	2023	12	66	0
1959	2024	13	66	2
1960	2025	14	66	4
1961	2026	15	66	6
1962	2027	16	66	8
1963	2028	17	66	10
1964	2029	18	67	0

1 Source: http://privatkunden.union-investment.de/handle?loadContent=/docme/service/faq/uniprofirente/2966812dae2d0486fe777a366e1f4afd.0.0/Grundsaetze_zur_Rente_mit_67.html (English Headings added by authors).

The actual amount one receives for retirement is determined by the **amount of time paid into the system** during the years worked. As a supplement that is **fundamentally voluntary**, there are company pension plans. Workers therefore have a right to have part of their wages or salary set aside to support a company pension plan that they can receive payments from upon retirement. With this a specific portion of an employee's gross annual income is converted into a company pension provision. The employer can choose between five options for carrying out company pension plans.

Question 343

What are the three pillars of a German retirement plan?

Answer

The three pillars are: 1

- state pension insurance,
- the company pension plan,
- the private pension plan, which often receives state-funded support.

Question 344

What is state pension insurance ("gesetzliche Rentenversicherung")?

Answer

The statutorily mandated pension insurance is based on the pay-as-you-go system. 2
That means that the contributions paid in are not save, instead they are immediately used for current pension payments for the retiree at that time. At the moment (2012) the contribution rate amounts to 19.5%, which is **split equally between the employee and employer**.

Question 345

Can state pension insurance be given up?

Answer

In general no as the state pension insurance is **mandatory**. Only in rare individual 3
cases are there exceptions.

Question 346

What is a company pension plan?

Answer

It is the promise of payment for the **purpose of maintenance**, one of the precipitat- 4
ing events for the claim to maintenance being age, disability or death and the con-

sent of an employee due to the employment relationship. Granting a company pension is **voluntary**, though. So long one is granted, the particulars are regulated by the German Company Pension Act.

Question 347

Which additional pension plan is common in Germany?

Answer

5 In Germany private pension plans **subsidized by the state** are common. They are concluded on a voluntary basis. Then there are the state-subsidized pension plans, the best known today being the **"Riester" pension**, named after its creator, *Walter Riester*, former Secretary of Labor and Social Affairs. These plans are **subsidized through extra pay**. Valuating the retirement plan provisions of the contribution for tax purposes is possible. The downside lies in the costly administration, which also leads to higher cost burdens of the "Riester" contracts in comparison to other forms of pension plans. For this reason weighing the difference between tax advantage, state subsidy, and higher costs must be considered. Besides, there is the **"Rürup" pension** plan, named after its creator, *Hans-Adalbert "Bert" Rürup*, former Secretary for Trade and Industry. This plan is a voluntary insurance that is on offer, especially for self-employed, freelance professionals and high earners.

Chapter 29 Right of Residency/Residency Permit Allowing for Employment/Visa | Aufenthaltsrecht/ Arbeitsgenehmigung/Visa

Definition, Legal Principles

!

The right of residency ("Aufenthaltsrecht") is part of the EU right to move freely. The legal basis of an EU citizen's right of residency in Germany is the EU Freedom of Movement Act of January 1, 2005. **EU citizens** with rights of free mobility and their EU family members do not require stay permits for either their entry into or residency in Germany, so they do not require a residency permit. Thus, the former temporary residency permit for EU citizens has been dropped since the EU Freedom of Movement Act came into force. From then on the only official form they received has been a certificate stating their right of residence, in accordance with sec. 5 of the EU Freedom of Movement Act. Further **citizens of the European Economic Area** (EEA) do not require permission of entry into and residency within Germany's borders. For **citizens of Switzerland** special regulations apply so that they require a stay permit within Germany's borders only. Members of other countries than mentioned require a permission of entry into and residency within Germany's borders usually. Such stay permits are granted as a visa, a residency permit, a settlement permit, an EU blue card or a permanent residence permit. These stay permits usually entitle its holder to work in Germany.

I. General Aspects

Question 348
Who counts as a foreigner under German law?

Answer
Simple: those who are not German. 1

Question 349
Which citizenships need a residency permit?

Answer
Citizenships from state that do not belong to the EU, EEA, or Switzerland. 2

Question 350
Who counts as EU citizens and enjoys the unrestricted free movement of workers ("Arbeitnehmerfreizügigkeit")?

Answer
Citizens of: Belgium, Denmark, Finland, France, Greece, Great Britain, Ireland, It- 3
aly, Luxemburg, Malta, The Netherlands, Austria, Portugal, Sweden, Spain and Cy-

prus, as well as (as of May 1, 2011) Estonia, Latvia, Lithuania, Poland, Slovenia, Slovakia, Czech Republic and Hungary.

Question 351
Who belongs to the European Economic Area (EEA)?

Answer
4 Non-European Union member states, such as Iceland, Norway and Liechtenstein belong to the EEA.

Question 352
What applies for Bulgarian, Croatian and Romanian citizens?

Answer
5 The free entrance in the German labor market will be opened for these citizenships at the end of a **transitional period**. With the transitional agreements anchored by the Treaty of Accession, this period **ends no later than December 31, 2013** for citizens of Bulgaria and Romania. The reduced speed at which Croatian workers can transition into the German labor market applies through June 30, 2015 and cannot be extended beyond any later than June 30, 2020. During these transitional periods Bulgarian, Croatian and Romanian citizens may only work with an EU residency permit that allows for employment ("Arbeitsgenehmigung-EU") and can only work for employers if they have such a permit.

Question 353
What applies to Swiss citizens?

Answer
6 Swiss citizens do not belong to the EEA but are **on equal terms with EEA citizens** per the Swiss-EU Agreement on the Free Movement of Persons.

Question 354
Which countries are described as non-members?

Answer
7 All countries other than Switzerland or that are not EU or EEA members are considered non-membership states.

Question 355
What is the unrestricted free movement of workers ("Arbeitnehmerfreizügigkeit") exactly?

Answer
Every EU citizen has the right to take on and perform work under the **same conditions as in his/her home country** regardless of his/her residency or citizenship. 8
The EU member state workers will be **treated equally** with respect to the profession or vocation, wages and other work conditions.

Question 356
Which registered stay permits ("Aufenthaltstitel") are there to differentiate from for employees?

Answer
There are: 9
- Visa ("Visum"),
- Residency Permit ("Aufenthaltserlaubnis/Aufenthaltsgenehmigung"),
- Residency Permit that Allows for Employment ("Aufenthaltserlaubnis/Aufenthaltsgenehmigung, die zur Erwerbstätigkeit berechtigt");
- Settlement Permit ("Niederlassungserlaubnis") and
- Permanent Residence Permit/Long-Term Resident's Permit ("Daueraufenthaltsberechtigung/langfristige Aufenthaltsberechtigung").

II. Visa

Question 357
Who needs a visa?

Answer
The Federal Foreign Office ("Auswärtiges Amt") provides on his website an overview on countries whose citizens need a visa.[1] Citizens of certain countries – for example Australia, Israel, Japan or the United States – are privileged and do not need a visa for entering Germany but they are not allowed to work without applying for work permit. These citizens may stay in Germany for a period up to 90 days per half 10

1 See http://www.auswaertiges-amt.de/EN/EinreiseUndAufenthalt/StaatenlisteVisumpflicht_node.html.

year without a visa. The non-EU/EEA foreigners who are not privileged need a visa to enter Germany.

Question 358

Who is responsible for the issuance of visas? What should one pay special attention to?

Answer

11 The German Embassy or Consulate in the applicant's home country is responsible for the issuance of visas. The applicant should get into contact with the **diplomatic mission abroad** about the intent to travel to Germany in a timely fashion. In order to avoid time-consuming queries, the applicant should **provide as many documents as possible.** That would include a valid passport, and, if the applicant is not applying from his/her home country, a valid residency permit.

Question 359

Other than the worker, who is allowed to enter Germany?

Answer

12 Beyond the worker him/herself, family members (**spouse and children**) are allowed to enter Germany. Requirements for granting the spouse a residences permit are that both spouses are at least 18 years of age, the spouse is able to communicate in the German language on a basic level at least and that the worker has a valid residence permit. For minor, unmarried children of the worker among others it is necessary that the worker has been granted a residence permit. In case of a minor, unmarried child who is 16 years of age or older it is necessary that this child has a strong command of the German language or it has to appear on the basis of the child's education and way of life to date that he or she will **be able to integrate into the way of life** which prevails in Germany. Other dependents of the worker may be granted a residence permit for the **purpose of subsequent immigration** to join the worker, if necessary in order to avoid particular hardship. Family members would need to apply for and receive a **limited or unlimited residency permit** ("Aufenthaltserlaubnis" or "Niederlassungserlaubnis"), demonstrate that they have sufficient housing with the given employee if they cannot afford their own. Further, there must be proof that typical living costs for the family members can be covered by employment, own savings/assets or other legal means.

Question 360

Who has to take care of the required permits?

Answer

The worker has to apply for the permit(s). The employer **can aid in the preparation** 13
of the application but is not required to do so.

III. Entrance to the German Labor Market

Question 361

According to what legal rule is entrance into the German labor market determined?

Answer

For the most part this includes the German Residence Act ("Aufenthaltsgesetz") and 14
the employment regulations and employment procedure regulations approved by via this law. Section 18 of the German Residence Act regulates the residency for employment purposes and requires the approval of the German Federal Employment Agency.

Question 362

When is entry into the German labor market possible for non-EU/EEA residents?

Answer

There has to be a **concrete job offer** and the foreigner may not be forced to work on 15
lower working conditions than those one would have to offer a German employee; there cannot be **any disadvantage to the German labor market**, i.e. there cannot be any German or foreign worker already in Germany that would be more preferable for the position.

Question 363

For which worker(s) is entry into the German labor market made easier?

Answer

Entry is made easier for **skilled personnel** and for the **highly qualified** – e.g. spe- 16
cialists – and academics. Highly qualified persons are, in particular scientists with special technical knowledge, teaching personnel in prominent positions or specialists with special professional experience who receive a salary equal to or exceeding the **contribution assessment ceiling of the general pension scheme.** A foreigner may be granted a residence permit for the purpose of studying at a state or state-recognized university or a comparable educational establishment. The residence permit entitles the holder to take up employment totaling no more than 90 days or 180 half-days per year, and to take up spare-time student employment. Further

foreigner may be issued a residence permit for the purpose of **basic and advanced industrial training**, if the Federal Employment Agency has granted approval.

IV. Residency Permit/Residency Permit with a Right to Work

Question 364
With which citizenship(s) would one not need a residency permit?

Answer
17 Citizenship in EU member states, the EEA and Switzerland enjoy an **unrestricted** free movement of workers.

Question 365
Is the residency permit with a right to work limited?

Answer
18 Yes, it has to be **renewed regularly**, since each residency permit is **tied to a reason** for the stay in Germany. The reason for an employee can be with the job he/she is doing.

Question 366
When does the residency with a right to work need to be applied for?

Answer
19 The application needs to have been made **prior to arrival** in Germany.

Question 367
Where does the application need to be made?

Answer
20 German Embassies and Consulates are responsible for the application.

Question 368
When does the residency with a right to work for citizens of visa-free nations (e.g. South Korea, Australia, USA, New Zealand, Japan, Israel and Canada) need to be applied for?

Answer

The application has to be applied for if the **stay will exceed three months** and before the work starts. The application can be made at the Foreigners' Registration Office ("Ausländerbehörde") after arrival in Germany. 21

Question 369

What applies regarding extending registered residence permits ("Aufenthaltstiteln")?

Answer

The worker is obligated to apply for an extension **three months prior** to the expiration of his/her registered residence permits. 22

Question 370

Does the employer have to pay the foreign worker for work performed if that foreigner does not have a registered residence permit?

Answer

No, because the lack of a registered stay permits **nullifies the employment contract**. And, from a nullified contract the employed person cannot assert a claim to compensation against the employer. 23

V. Work Permit

Question 371

When does a foreign worker need a work permit?

Answer

A worker from a non-EU/EEA nation requires the issuance of a work permit if he/she plans to accept work in Germany. 24

Question 372

Who is responsible for issuing the testing that determines who may receive a work permit?

Answer

The Central Placement Office of the Federal Employment Agency ("Zentrale Auslands- und Fachvermittlung – ZAV") is responsible for this. In **using a set stan-** 25

dard, the Central Placement Office of the Federal Employment Agency tests Germany-wide and decides whether a non-EU/EEA citizen can be issued a work permit or not.

Question 373

Who is responsible for the issuance of work permits?

Answer

26 If the worker can travel **without a visa**, the local Foreigners' Registration Office at the place where the worker has his residence in Germany is responsible. If a **visa obligation** exists, the German embassy or consulate in the worker's respective country is to be contacted.

Question 374

When does a work permit need to be applied for?

Answer

27 A work permit has to be applied for **prior to arrival** in Germany if a **visa obligation** exists. The agreement of the German Federal Employment Agency ("Bundesagentur für Arbeit") or the Central Placement Office of the Federal Employment Agency ("Zentrale Auslands- und Fachvermittlung – ZAV") has to be presented. The agreement of the local Foreigners' Registration Office at the place where the worker plans his residence in Germany is necessary basically. If the worker can travel **without a visa**, applying after arrival suffices.

Question 375

What applies for workers from EU/EEA member states?

Answer

28 They are treated the same as German citizens in this respect and do not require a special work permit. To them the **unrestricted free movement** of workers applies and they can **pursue every type of profession** in Germany. An exception applies to Bulgarians, Croatians and Romanians. The free access to the German labor market will be made possible at the end of a transitional period. That period ends on December 31, 2013 for Bulgarian and Romanian employees and no later than June 30, 2020 for Croatian employees.

Question 376
What consequences does the employer who employs a foreigner without a work permit have to expect?

Answer
Employers may only employ foreign workers who hold a registered stay permit. Vio- 29
lations of this represent a **regulatory offense** and the impending **sanctions** for such actions include fines or imprisonment. The regulatory offense can be penalized with a fine of up to 500,000 €.

Question 377
What consequences does the worker have to expect for violations of this nature?

Answer
The worker may be incur a fine of up to 5,000 €. It can lead to being **forced to leave** 30
Germany. Further, the worker in this situation will not receive pay for his/her work and cannot register for German social security benefits.

Question 378
Which obligations exist for the employer who employs a foreigner without a work permit?

Answer
An employer is **obligated to check** if the employee possesses the proper working 31
papers. The employer is **obligated to store a copy of the permit** in electronic or paper form.

Chapter 30 Severance Agreement | Aufhebungsvertrag

Definition, Legal Principles

By way of a severance agreement an employment relationship is **ended by mutual agreement** without the observance of any grace period. As with a dismissal notice, a severance agreement must be in writing. Often found in severance agreements are **lump-sum severance payments** that are intended to compensate for the loss of employment as well as rules about the furnishing of a reference or payment in lieu of vacation time that can be affected.

One needs to differentiate, however, between a severance agreement and a **contract-finalizing agreement** ("Abwicklungsvertrag"). The latter form of agreement exists in cases when notice of termination has already been given and only the other modalities will be arranged. In such an agreement, rules about possible severance payments or the like can be arranged. A contract-finalizing agreement is further, a two-sided contractual provision and the employer has already terminated the employment agreement.

Question 379

Is there an obligation to conclude a severance agreement in Germany?

Answer

1 No. Employers and employees may **freely** decide if they want to adhere to the employment contract or conclude a severance agreement.[1]

Question 380

When is a severance agreement normally concluded?

Answer

2 The conclusion of an employment contract provides an opportunity to terminate an employment contract on **as short of notice and risk-free as possible**.

Question 381

What are the advantages to a severance agreement for the employer?

Answer

3 A severance agreement is not subject to any collective bargaining or employment termination laws. The employment contract can be terminated without observing legal, collective bargaining or individual contractually stipulated notice periods. General

1 For situations where the employer wants to end the working relationship and the employee does not, see Chapter 7.

and special dismissal protections have no application. Policies for the protection of pregnant women, young mothers and severely handicapped persons need not to be observed. The **conditions** of the severance agreement **can be freely negotiated**.

Question 382

What are the advantages of a severance agreement for the employee?

Answer

The shortening of the notification period allows for the possibility to assume **work with another employer immediately**. If the employee is guilty of serious misconduct that results in immediate dismissal for cause, an **"unsuspicious" date of termination** can be set with the severance agreement. The conditions can be freely negotiated. 4

Question 383

What are the linguistic considerations regarding a severance agreement in the German language for a foreigner?

Answer

The foreigner has to have a good command of German or the explanation of the employer has **to be translated** for him or her. 5

Question 384

What is the difference between a severance agreement and a limited-term employment agreement?

Answer

A severance agreement and limited-term employment agreement differs in that the **termination of the employment is not a component** of the employment contract, but instead will be agreed to upon the signing of it. 6

Question 385

What has to be arranged in a severance agreement? Is there a minimum content requirement?

Answer

The sole content item required in a severance agreement is the agreement of the parties about the termination of the employment relationship. The time at which that 7

relationship is terminated may be freely negotiated. If this is missing, the employment contract will be **terminated with immediate effect.** An employment contract that is not yet or not already again in place **can be retroactively ended.** Note that a severance agreement has to regulate the following:
- leave of absence,
- vacation time,
- severance pay,
- retirement benefits,
- company car,
- employer loans, and
- settlement clause.

Question 386
Which regulations would be advisable for a severance agreement?

Answer
8 In the severance agreement, the following issues can be regulated:
- compensation,
- official wording,
- career consulting,
- duty of notification,
- references, and
- discretion.

Question 387
May severance agreements be hidden in an addendum to the employment contract?

Answer
9 No, it may not be. Indeed this deals with an unusual provision. This will not become part of the contract because, according to the outward appearance of the contract, the employee does **not have to expect such clauses.**

Question 388
Does the severance agreement have to be in writing?

Answer
10 Yes, the law stipulates it to be in written form. The requirement to have it in writing is **compulsory**, not optional.

Question 389

Is a scanned-in signature legally valid?

Answer

No, the electronic form is precluded from severance agreements. The severance agreement has to be **signed by hand in original** by both parties. The reason for this is that the law for severance agreements stipulates handwritten and not merely written form, the latter including photocopies, scans, etc. 11

Question 390

Who has to sign the severance agreement?

Answer

The employer and the employee have to sign the agreement for it to have legal force. The employer can, however, **appoint a proxy**. It is legally insufficient if only one side signs the termination offer provided by the other party, with or without the addition of a clause stating that both parties have agreed. In case of identical versions it suffices to have signed the version of the other party; the signer does not need to retain a copy with his own signature. The version with the **original signature** must be handed over, as a mere copy of the signed copy is not enough. 12

Question 391

Can the foreign parent company sign the severance agreement?

Answer

The foreign parent company can only sign the severance agreement **if it has been authorized** to do so. 13

Question 392

How much time to consider the agreement does the employer have to grant the employee?

Answer

The employee is to be granted a reasonable amount of time for due consideration. As a rule a reasonable amount of time to consider would mean **two weeks.** In special situations, as with vacation or difficulty reaching an attorney, the time to consider **may be extended** to four weeks. 14

Question 393
Does the employer have to assume the employee's legal fees?

Answer
15 No, the employee covers them him/herself. Should the employee have insurance that includes legal expenses, these costs would be covered so long as the severance agreement disputes to be settled using the employee's legal expenses insurance are covered by the policy. This is then the case if the employee does **not voluntarily decide on the conclusion** of the severance agreement.

Question 394
Does the employer have a duty to disclose information?

Answer
16 No, it will be assumed that the employee will inform him/herself about consequences prior to the conclusion of the severance agreement. The employer is therefore **not obligated to point out detrimental consequences**. If the severance agreement has come about on the employer's initiative and in his/her interest, an increased duty to disclose may apply to the employer.

Question 395
What is a contract-finalizing agreement ("Abwicklungsvertrag")?

Answer
17 In a contract-finalizing agreement the parties **agree on the conditions after a dismissal** to which the employee resigns. Different than a severance agreement, the contract-finalizing agreement does not affect the conditions of the employment relationship alone. The employment relationship is ended by the employer terminating beforehand.

Chapter 31 Severance Pay | Abfindung

Definition, Legal Principles

! In Germany payment of severance is an acknowledged means of consensually ending employment relationships. This is done by a severance agreement or reaching a similar agreement, unless it is a special case within the context of restructuring, the closing of the company/plant or part of it. There is, however, **no statutory obligation** to pay severance in Germany. In section 1a of the German Protection Against Dismissal Act ("Kündigungsschutzgesetz – KSchG"), legislators have provided employers with the chance to offer their employees a **legally fixed minimum severance** if the employee waives his/her right to litigate for protection from unfair dismissal. In Germany socially balanced layoff plans in cases of restructuring regularly contain severance payment agreements, as one also finds in both actual and legally challenging special cases that represent an **increased risk of litigation** to the employer. Further still, contracts on the executive and upper management level are commonly dissolved with severance agreements in cases of early termination of employment by the company. The amount of the severance is not codified in German law, as the **amount is very much an individual matter.** For simple cases, German labor courts have developed a basic operand of 1/2-month's salary for each year of service to the company. Legislatively speaking, section 1a of the German Protection Against Dismissal Act has also oriented itself to this measure. Yet severance payments ranging from 1/4 to 1-1/4 of a month's salary are just as common in Germany.

Question 396

Must the employer pay severance[1] at the end of the employment relationship?

Answer

Principally speaking, German law does not require the payment of severance benefits with the exception of section 1a of the German Employment Protection Act. However, a severance pay is common upon dismissal. It can be **freely negotiated** between the employer and employee in the same way that the employer and works council or union can with a socially balanced layoff plan. In the context of dismissal litigation, severance pay is **often paid at the conclusion of the litigation.** 1

Question 397

What does the regulation laid out in section 1a of the German Protection Against Dismissal Act mean with dismissal due to operational reasons ("betriebsbedingte Kündigung")?

Answer

Under this law, the employee has the **right to severance pay** if the employer supports dismissal due to urgent operational reasons in writing and freely explains that 2

1 For severance agreements, see Chapter 30.

the employee can claim the severance pay, after allowing the right to file a claim to expire. An estimate of the severance pay is unnecessary. This German Employment law mandates that the amount of the severance pay be **0.5 months salary for each year of employment**. Reason: The simplification of dismissal due to operational reasons and reduction of risk of litigation for the employer.

Question 398
Can the German Labor Court unilaterally establish severance pay within the framework of litigation for wrongful termination ("Kündigungsschutzprozess")?

Answer
3 No. The court can, however, submit a proposed agreement and achieve an agreement through those means.

Question 399
Are there exceptions in this regard?

Answer
4 Yes, there is a possibility of dissolving the employment relationship in return for a compensation payment by request from the parties. In the framework of a protection against dismissal procedure the invalidity of the dismissal has to have been established. The request **requires the reasoning** for it. An exception exists for upper management.

Question 400
On average, how high is severance pay in Germany?

Answer
5 In Germany on average the employee receives severance pay in the amount of **a half-month's salary for each year of employment** according to statistics and surveys.

Question 401
When will the severance pay from a severance agreement be paid?

Answer
6 Normally, the **determined end of the employment relationship** marks the point in time that severance needs to be paid.

Question 402

When will severance pay be paid out with a settlement based on a court's cancellation agreement decision?

Answer

With a severance settlement based on a court's cancellation agreement decision, the point in time when severance pay is due cannot have been pre-determined. The point in time can **be based on the circumstances**. Normally, that particular point in time is marked by the employment relationship's end. 7

Question 403

Will severance pay be taxed by German authorities?

Answer

Yes, but the **tax rate varies** for each individual case. 8

Question 404

Is there a threat of losing unemployment benefit during a so-called blocking period ("Sperrzeit")?

Answer

Severance pay remains **disregarded with subsequent unemployment** in cases of an ordinary dismissal. The condition for this is that the notice period is observed. In all other cases with a severance agreement there is always a danger that the termination agreement will be construed as a voluntary ending of the employment relationship. In this case there is the risk of a **twelve-week blocking period**. Note: unemployment compensation is suspended for no longer than one year. 9

Question 405

Are severance payments from termination agreements inheritable?

Answer

Yes. The pre-condition for the inheritability is, however, that the employee has submitted and **signed the petition for termination him/herself** and died after the severance pay is due. 10

Question 406

Are severance payments from a court's cancellation agreement decision inheritable?

Answer

11 Yes, as described prior.

Question 407

Are severance payments from of a severance settlement and from a court's cancellation agreement decision transferable?

Answer

12 Yes. The severance payment arises from the settlement, which has **binding effect**, and by a decision that **has legal force**. The advance assignment of rights is permissible.

Chapter 32 Strike | Streik

Definition, Legal Principles

!

Constitutionally speaking, the right to strike in Germany is enshrined in Article 9, para. 3 of the "Grundgesetz", the "Basic Law". Though there is not statute on striking, this constitutional provision does afford the right a **special sort of protection**. The basis for the right to strike is therefore formed within the framework of **case law**. As a rule, a job action by employees is striking, while the means available to the employer is a **lockout** ("Aussperrung"). In 2011, 158 companies were directly affected by strikes.[1] In the following year, 1.2 million workers were recorded has having gone on strike.[2]

Strikes do not principally lead to violation of employment agreements. In accordance with German case law, the **rights and obligations of an employment relationship are merely suspended**. The case law states that a strike is only permissible with consideration of whether it goes too far in limiting a fundamental right ("Übermaßverbot"). Accordingly, strikes have to be **necessary and proportional** ("verhältnismäßig"). It is therefore normally considered necessary and proportional if prior negotiation efforts been exhausted have failed, or at least their failure is impending.

In Germany a **lockout** is when the employer prevents employees from coming to work and refuses to pay wages in accordance with a **preannounced plan**. A lockout can affect all company employees or be aimed only at those striking unwilling to perform their work-related tasks. As a rule, only after employees have commenced a strike will the employer imitate a lockout.

Question 408

What counts as a strike?

Answer

There is a strike if a large number of employees collectively and in a planned fashion **organized by a union** discontinue performing the work they are contracted to do to reach a common goal, **with the intent of starting to work again** once their period of the refusal to work has drawn to a close. 1

Question 409

Is the right to carry out a strike regulated by law?

Answer

The concept of a strike (labor dispute) is neither expressly regulated by law nor is an express basic right to strike provided for. Article 9, para. 3 of the German Basic Law (constitutional document) may be derived from a **constitutional guaranty** to labor 2

1 See http://de.statista.com/statistik/daten/studie/218785/umfrage/anzahl-der-von-streik-betroffenen-betriebe-in-deutschland.

2 See http://de.statista.com/statistik/daten/studie/221563/umfrage/arbeitskaempfe-streikende-ausgefallene-arbeitstage.

disputes. Further still, the expression "labor dispute" ("Arbeitskampf") is used in numerous other German statutes.

Question 410

Who possesses the right to strike?

Answer

3 Each and **every employee** possesses the right to strike. The entity of the trade union responsible for organizing the strike also possesses the right to strike.

Question 411

What is the objective of a strike?

Answer

4 The objective is the enforcement of the **striker's own demands**. Here, a lock-out is the means of pressure the employer uses, while a strike is the classic measure used by workers. A strike serves as means of **settling regulatory difficulties and solving conflicts**. If a peaceful understanding between contractual partners fails, adversarial negotiating partners can be put under pressure by the application of collective measures.

Question 412

What different kinds of strikes are there?

Answer

5 There are warning strikes, defensive strikes, sympathy strikes (secondary actions), general strikes, full strikes, across-the-board strikes, partial strikes, rolling strikes, demonstration strikes, political strikes, successive strikes, strikes in waves, and "go-slow" strikes.

Question 413

By which principles is a strike characterized?

Answer

6 Labor disputes are marked by equality and state neutrality. What is meant with **equality** is the promotion of equal opportunity of contractual partners to actively participate in creating the contract. **State neutrality** refers to the state not influencing actual negotiations so as to sway the balance between the contracting parties.

Question 414
Can an employee be compelled to strike?

Answer
No, the employee has to decide if he/she wishes to participate in a strike. The employee **cannot be subjected** to a strike or forced to stop working against his/her will. 7

Question 415
Is membership in the union organizing the strike necessary for participating in the strike?

Answer
No, as even employees that do not belong to the striking union – or any other, for that matter – can take part in the strike. This understanding arises from the **principle of workforce and company unity**. 8

Question 416
Can minors participate in strikes?

Answer
Yes, as the **authorization from the youth's legal guardian** for him or her to work includes that youth's permission to strike as well under German law. 9

Question 417
Can trainees and apprentices participate in strikes?

Answer
According to German Federal Labor Court precedent trainees and apprentices possess a right to participate in **a short, time-limited strike** (e.g. warning strike). 10

Question 418
Can a works council member participate in a strike in his capacity of employee?

Answer
Yes, but **special rules** apply in light of his function as representative for the interests of those who continue to be employed at the company. 11

Question 419

May a works council member participate in a strike on behalf of the company's interests?

Answer

12 Principally, the position on the works council is neither canceled nor paused. It behooves works council member to abide by their obligation to **remain peaceful and neutral** as set out in the Works Constitution Act, whereby the works council member is not allowed to use that office to legally bring a labor dispute.

Question 420

May senior management/executives participate in strikes?

Answer

13 Yes, as German law does not differentiate between striking senior management/executives and other striking employees.

Question 421

Can board members participate in strikes?

Answer

14 No, members of legal entities' representative bodies are recognized for their **commercial status** and are not employees despite any employment contract they may have.

Question 422

Can civil servants participate in strikes?

Answer

15 No, as civil servants, judges and soldiers follow a **strike ban** based on an understanding of civil service in the German constitutional document, the "Grundgesetz".

Question 423

May public sector employees participate in strikes?

Answer

16 Yes, as German law does not recognize them as civil servants. In employment dispute matters they are directed to negotiate their work conditions at the **collective bargaining agreement level**.

Question 424
When is a strike legal?

Answer
German law does not clearly lay out when a strike is legal. The legality of labor disputes has to be inferred from German Federal Labor Court **case law**. Ostensibly, there is an understood obligation to **keep the peace**. However, that obligation comes to a close with the end of the collective bargaining agreement. At that point management and labor can take a job action in order to pressure the other party regarding their demands. 17

Question 425
What prevailing circumstances have to exist in order for a strike to be legal?

Answer
A strike has to be the **last means of negotiation** (in legalese, the ultima ratio) and the time for adhering to the obligation to keep the peace cannot have expired. Further, there has to be an **adoption of a resolution** by the given labor union. For this a decision by the board of the given organizational body is required. 18

Question 426
What content does the resolution adopted have to contain?

Answer
The resolution adopted has to be made known and contain the following about the strike: 19
- objective,
- when it is to begin,
- type, and
- scope.

Question 427
What are the legal consequences of an illegal strike?

Answer
If an employee participates in an illegal strike, his contractual obligations to perform the given job are not complied with. However, the employer has a legally enforceable right to performance of the work. Thus, the employee **loses a right to compensation**, as the strike action frees the employer from having to pay wages. In 20

fact, the employer can **terminate the employee** due to the latter's failure to perform his contractual obligations. Furthermore, the illegal strike provides grounds for comprehensive contractual claims and tort liability.

Question 428
What limits are there on the power to strike?

Answer
21 **Criminal law** is deemed to be the limiting factor. Occupation, boycotts and blockades of the workplace are impermissible, as well as bodily harm or property damage.

Chapter 33 Traineeship | Praktikum

Definition, Legal Principles

!

The German term "Praktikant", in English trainee, or, in some cases, internship, for the most part comprised of and defined by the German Vocational Training Act ("Berufsbildungsgesetz"). Section 26 of this law defines a trainee as a person who **temporarily undertakes specific work and training** that is related to company needs. Though that work will be within the rubric and context of a complete company training, a traineeship does not require completion of a systematic vocational training, as the traineeship is required to have several specific purposes. These include among other purposes: admittance to university-level study, certain examinations for the given profession.

This form of work offers **attractive opportunities** not only for the particular proprietor/company but also the particular trainee. To begin with, such arrangements offer both parties what is a usually mutually agreed upon temporary **chance to learn whether they can or cannot work together** without having to make a long term employment commitment. Additionally, the trainee can begin **making the business contacts** necessary for the advance of his/her career, and the **proprietor/company can check early** on if the particular trainee is a good fit for a future job at that company or for that proprietor.

Question 429

What is the difference between a trainee and employment relationship under German law?

Answer

In a traineeship, the education and training is the primary aim. Accordingly, train- 1
eeship and employment relationships are differentiated by the fact that the primary goal of a traineeship is for the trainee **to gain business experience and skills,** while the employment relationship's primary goal is the **exchange of service for remuneration.**

Question 430

How is the divide between traineeships and other work relationships in Germany made?

Answer

The **manner in which work is carried out** is what controls the interpretative defi- 2
nition under German law. It does not depend on how the parties classify the contractual relationship. For the relationship to be legally considered a traineeship, a rough classification or delineation to this effect must be made by comparing the **portion of the "educational purpose"** ("Ausbildungszweck"). Further, the services rendered and work for the company can be placed within the context and are a result of the emphasis being placed on practical experience and learning.

Further, a traineeship relationship exists only if the **overriding emphasis is on** 3
educational purposes and company's imparting of experience of skills to the

trainee. Legal relationships that **do not serve to further develop the trainee** but instead only the completion of incidental work are regularly considered employment and not traineeships.

Question 431

Why is the differentiation between the various types of work relationships so important?

Answer

4 Depending on what the legal relationship is considered to be, as a rule, **different legal frameworks** with different legal consequences exist. Accordingly, a precise classification is essential in order to guarantee a legally compliant application of the legal relationship.

5 Should a traineeship that is in fact an employment relationship actually be carried out, **all rights and responsibilities** arising from it being an employment relationship will have to be fully taken into account.

6 If the work of the trainee is possibly on the basis of a so-called "Scheinpraktikantenvertrag", a contractual "traineeship" agreement **in name only**, and the "trainee", at the employer's behest, works for a longer time period in a fashion that does not serve the educational and professional training of the "trainee" but instead **serves the company's needs** considerably more, that "trainee" is **entitled to compensation** in accordance with sec. 612 of the German Commercial Code. The amount of remuneration is based on the existence of a specific remuneration rate, which is set by federal or state law; in want of a remuneration rate, the **amount would be set in accordance with the typical pay rate** for the given job.

Question 432

What are the principle demands made in a traineeship contract?

Answer

7 The design of a trainee contract should always adhere to the **subject and aim of the traineeship**. It should be stressed here that how the transfer of practical experience and how skills are attained **is a priority** in order to ensure the differentiation between a traineeship and employment relationship.

Question 433

Do general German employment regulations and legal principles apply to a trainee relationship?

Answer

Yes, and the general employment regulations and legal principles in the sense of the German Vocational Training Act apply. In this context, the German Federal Paid Leave, Continuation of Remuneration and the Working Hours Acts are to be noted. According to these laws, trainees are entitled to **paid vacation, holiday pay** and **continued remuneration when out sick**. 8

Question 434

Is there a requirement for trainee contracts to be in writing?

Answer

If there is a traineeship relationship in the sense of the German Vocational Training Act, the parties may forgo a **memorandum of contract**. That said, a contract in **written form is recommended** as a means of facilitating the giving of evidence in cases of disagreement. 9

Question 435

Does the duration of the traineeship have to be adhered to?

Answer

Yes, a traineeship relationship in terms of the German Vocational Training Act has to be **limited in time** and regulated by contract. The traineeship principally ends following the end of the limited term. 10

Question 436

Is it possible to end a traineeship early?

Answer

Yes, but an early termination is only possible when the conditions set out in German Vocational Training Act are met; while the presence of this is, for the proprietor/company, basically **for presenting good cause**. On the other hand the trainee can quit his/her traineeship by **giving four weeks notice** if the trainee chooses so. 11

Question 437

Can a traineeship be prevented from leading to an employment relationship with the same company?

Answer

12 No, as legal precedent informs us that trainee relationship is **not viewed as an employment relationship** in the sense of the German Act on Part-Time Work and Fixed-Term Employment and therefore does not prevent the creation of a new fixed term. This is based on the purpose and sense of the Part-time Work and Fixed-term Employment Contracts Act, which suggests that **easing entry into the workforce is especially for newcomers.**

Question 438

Is there a legal requirement to remunerate trainees?

Answer

13 Yes, an employer who wishes to bring a trainee into the organization should think about that trainee's pay. It is about the remuneration not for the work performed but instead a sort of **subsistence expense reimbursement or allowance**. With the amount of the remuneration, there are individual cases to consider in which the aspects of the work performed on the one hand and the function of the allowance for subsistence on the other have some influence on the setting of remuneration.

Question 439

Do the rights granted by the German Works Constitution Act ("Betriebsverfassungsgesetz") apply to trainees?

Answer

14 Yes, the German Works Constitution Act **applies to all legal relationships** that, due to a contract governed by private law under which traineeships fall, impart professional knowledge, skills and experience.

15 Trainees are therefore entitled to **vote in elections** for or **run for office** in the works council.

Question 440

How long is the probationary period for trainees?

Answer

16 Differing to a vocational training relationship, a trainee probationary period may be agreed upon that is **at least one and no more than four months**; but a shorter, and not a longer, probationary period can also be agreed upon. Within this time period either the company or the trainee can end the traineeship relationship **without notice**.

Question 441

Does the trainee have the legal right to a reference letter?

Answer

Yes, even a trainee is entitled to a reference letter. When the traineeship ends or if one party ends the agreement, the trainee is **entitled to a written reference**. The reference has to contain type, duration and aim of the training and work, as well as the professional skills, knowledge and experience acquired by the trainee. 17

At the request of the trainee, **information about the behavior and accomplishments** are also to be included. 18

Question 442

What is an industrial placement or internship for school-aged children ("Betriebs-/ Schülerpraktikum") understood to be in Germany?

Answer

An industrial placement or internship for school-aged children is a sort of internship whose program and follow-up is **prepared by a school** and which is meant to help young people in the process of **choosing a career path** with an introduction to the business world. The program consists of a school event run at a business in which the **teacher acts as the traineeship supervisor**, and the implementation of the "traineeship" is coordinated in cooperation with a company contact person. 19

Neither a traineeship or employment relationship with the proprietor/company is established through such a program. 20

Question 443

In regards to the use of university-student interns, are there special points to consider?

Answer

Yes. If an internship is completed within the framework of a university program, the German Vocational Training Act does not apply. The contractual relationship is **subject to special rules:** 21

- A university students' internship contract should incorporate the fact that practical phases are a required and are to be completed during the time of studies and above all else serves to convey to the student job-related content and foster a deeper understanding of what is taught in the classroom.
- The proprietor/company is not required to pay interns. Any remuneration would be at the discretion of the proprietor/company.

- For a university-level intern, there is no entitlement to paid vacation, holiday pay or continued remuneration when out sick.
- University-level interns are not covered by the scope of laws against unfair dismissal. It would nevertheless be appropriate to include a provision in the intern's contract that regulates early termination and other rules on termination. This, however, should be only for serious breaches of duty, ones that lead to the internship being unreasonable to continue.
- The application of rights granted by the German Works Constitution Act depends on the given situation and the particular degree program. If, during the internship, the university-level intern finds him/herself in a status protected by private law, he/she is a regular vocational trainee in the sense of rights granted by the German Works Constitution Act and that law therefore applies.
- Should a university student offer his/her work for remuneration and that work is not part of a set internship program that is built into the student's plan of study, he/she is to be considered a working student worker and qualifies as an employee.

Chapter 34 Typical Employment Contract Content | Typische Arbeitsvertragsinhalte

Definition, Legal Principles

Employer and employee can principally form the terms of the contract freely. The German Law on Notification of Conditions Governing an Employment Relationship ("Nachweisgesetz") provides a guide to what **minimum content** legislators have stipulated and will want to have put into writing. This includes, for example, names of the employment contract partners, workplace location, scope and amount of vacation time as well as the amount and definition of duties to be performed. Beyond these basic rules are the **practical questions of interest**, such as those regarding employer loans, making company property available, usage of company automobiles, etc. Here, contractual partners can negotiate freely so long as no valid works or collective bargaining agreement states otherwise.

Question 444

Does the employer have to make a PC, mobile phone, and the like available to the employee?

Answer

The employer is obligated to make available all work and occupational safety 1
equipment necessary for the employee to carry out the job required of him/her. This includes office supplies.

Question 445

Does the employer have to allow the private usage of PCs, mobile devices, and the like?

Answer

No, this is not required. Different regulations apply if such consent is provided in an 2
individual employment contract or collective bargaining agreement.

Question 446

Does the employer have to pay for length-of-service bonuses or employee participation programs?

Answer

No, as no such obligation exists. Different rules apply if such payments are allowed 3
by an individual employment contract or a collective bargaining agreement. A claim to payment of an **anniversary bonus** exists when **a company norm is established** through repeated payments of this sort.

Question 447
May the employee pursue secondary employment?

Answer
4 Yes, so long as the employment relationship with the primary employer is not impaired and the legal cap on hours worked daily does not exceed ten hours. The employer can only **prohibit** an employee from taking on secondary employment **for legitimate interests** and then refuses to grant the consent required. A recognized legitimate interest for the employer is work at a rival company.

Question 448
Does the employer have to grant employee loans?

Answer
5 No, the employer does not. However, different rules apply if they are provided for by an individual employment contract or a collective bargaining agreement, something which **is uncommon.**

Question 449
May employees take on roles of honorary office?

Answer
6 Yes, so long as the role **does not prevent or make entirely impossible** the completion of his/her normal work.

Question 450
May an employee get involved in political, religious or trade union organizations?

Answer
7 Yes, so long as the role **neither disturbs operations** at the workplace **nor prevents the completion of work** by employees.

Question 451
Can an employer assign an employee to work at a different site, perform different work or both?

Answer

Such transfer, or relocation clauses are regularly found in employment contracts. What is decisive here is if the clause is **proportional and reasonable** to the employee. 8

Question 452

Can an employer post an employee at another affiliate or company within their group?

Answer

Yes, so long as the given employment contract also allows for other affiliates and companies within the group to be arranged as work-sites. According to the German Temporary Employment Act, an internal transfer **does not require permission** if the employee is not going to be hired and employed for the purpose of being permanently transferred. 9

Question 453

May the employer release the employee from having to work?

Answer

No, since along with the obligation to perform the work to be carried out comes the right to provide these services. The employer **has to provide work** for the employee and not solely pay him/her wages. This right is derived from the right to protection of one's individual sphere of life. The employer may only release the employee from having to work if the interest of the release from work is greater than the employer's interest for the performance of the work to be carried out. For instance this is the case with **valid dismissals for operational reasons** and the discontinuation of employment opportunity due to **restructuring**. The right to release from work because of dismissal can be explicitly agreed upon in the employment contract. 10

Question 454

What needs to be observed with respect to business trips?

Answer

Employees are obligated to go on business trips if the employment contract includes them. This obligation does not have to be expressly agreed upon. It can **arise out of the job description or line of work**. The employer can also mandate business trips as part of his/her authority to give instructions per the obligations set out in the employment contract. 11

Question 455
Are employees entitled to a company car?

Answer
12 No, unless the employee is granted a company car by contract. However, from the perspective of the German Employment law **principle of equal treatment**, the employee can be entitled to a company car if his co-workers in the same position have one.

Question 456
May the employee have a company car for private use?

Answer
13 No, this is not required. Different regulations apply if such consent is provided in an individual employment contract or collective bargaining agreement.

Question 457
Does the employer have to approve or possibly pay for an employee to pursue further professional training?

Answer
14 No, as no such legal obligation exists. The employer's obligation to approve or pay for further professional training **can be the result of stipulations** in an employment contract or collective bargaining or works agreement. If such a stipulation is missing, a right can arise out of the **principle of equal treatment** if the employer has approved training for employees in the same position.

Question 458
If the employer pays for the further professional training, can he/she oblige the employee to reimburse these costs upon resignation?

Answer
15 That depends whether the employee **gained an added value** from the professional training, how expensive it was and for how long it lasted. A reimbursement clause has to take into account the level and duration of the reimbursement payments.

Question 459
Are employees entitled to company housing?

Answer

No, but usage of a company housing can be promised to the employee in an employment contract. The right of use is then a **part of the compensation package**. In this case the termination of an employment contract cannot be isolated from the lease agreement. 16

Question 460

What are preclusion periods?

Answer

Preclusion periods (aka "expiration periods" – "Verfallsfristen") can be found in employment contracts, collective bargaining agreements and works agreements. **Agreed to or statutorily protected rights expire** by way of preclusion periods if assertion of the rights does not take place within the agreed time period and in the agreed form. Preclusion periods serve in this respect to **shorten the three-year statutory limitation period** that arises in employment relationships. Preclusion periods are **to be observed officially through the courts** without one party having to rely on it. They therefore hold a stronger and more detrimental effect for the affected party than the statute of limitations. 17

Question 461

What can employers do against the illicit communication of (company) secrets?

Answer

Employers usually protect themselves with **employment contract clauses** that obligate the employer to secrecy with respect to company and trade secrets. This obligation to secrecy begins with the signing of the employment contract and **does not end after the end of the employment relationship**. The employer can also conclude a **special non-disclosure agreement** ("Geheimhaltungsvertrag"). This is subject to criminal law protection. In cases of illicit communication of a (company) secret, employees can be subject to **three years imprisonment**. Furthermore, the employer can explicitly state the need for secrecy or protect the corresponding files with passwords. 18

Question 462

Does an employer operating in Germany have to establish a company-run daycare center?

Answer

19 No, as no such legal obligation exists in this respect. Different regulations apply if such consent is provided in an individual employment contract or collective bargaining agreement.

Question 463

Does the employer have to offer company sports activities or a gym?

Answer

20 No, as no such legal obligation exists on this issue. Different regulations apply if such amenities are to be provided for per an individual employment contract or collective bargaining agreement.

Question 464

Does the employer have to offer perks or benefits like "Jobtickets" (for public transportation), reduced-cost lunches or health exams?

Answer

21 No, as **no such legal obligation exists** in this respect. Different regulations apply if consent is provided in an individual employment contract or collective bargaining agreement.

Question 465

To what extent does the employer have duty to provide health care and benefits?

Answer

22 The general duty to provide health care and benefits that employers have obligates them to act accordingly, as "employer", meaning that they have to keep the employee's interest in mind, safeguarding the company's interest and that of other employees in a way that appears correct and fair in view of the **principle of good faith**. This is determined by the **need for protection** of each employee, which increases with a view to the length of service to the company or the position of trust. The duty to provide health care and benefits begins taking effect **during the contract negotiation phase**, with issues like the duty to explain the employee-employer relationship to be expected. Furthermore, there is a legal duty to explain how German social security works, and the employer has a responsibility for employee welfare that includes providing leave for job search, information about former employees, issuance of working papers as well as the preparation of references. The employer is also committed to the **care of the em-**

ployee's life and health. He/she has to **avert avoidable disadvantages** to the employee.

Question 466
What duties of fidelity exist for the employee?

Answer
Out of employment, an employee has an **obligation to work**. There are also secondary obligations for the employee in order to safeguard the protection-worthy interests of the employer. There are individual restrictive covenants, but also obligations to carry out favorable actions. The employee may not share with a third party any trade or company secrets. Based on the employee **obligation of secrecy and non-disclosure**, the employee is to refrain from communicating information that could harm one's reputation or credit. The employee **may not accept bribes** ("handshake money"). Further, the employee **may not compete** with his/her employer in the employer's given area of business. Employees are also affected by their duties to disclose and report about matters such as a pending loss. In addition to this, the employee has a **duty to obey the employer**. 23

Question 467
Can an employee refuse to perform work?

Answer
Without a special reason, basically not. A refusal to perform work can entitle the employer to **terminate the employment contract** and **demand damages**. That said the employee is entitled to refuse to do work if he/she finds him/herself in a situation where performing the given task may be actually possible but the employer cannot demand fulfillment of the task due to **overriding aspects**. An example of this would be if the employee finds himself in a moral conflict due to the work to be performed. 24

Question 468
Are employees entitled to a part-time work?

Answer
Yes, but a requirement for this is that the employee has been working for the given employer for **at least six months**. The application for part-time work can only be made **biennially**. 25

Question 469

When do claims arising out of an employment contract come under the statute of limitations and expire?

Answer

26 The statutes of limitations run from three months to **as long as thirty years**. After three months, all employer claims regarding the employee's anti-competition violations against the employer because of the employer's knowledge of the business lapse. After thirty years the statute of limitations for claims for return of property expires regarding ownership and other property rights. However, the **general statute of limitations is three years**.

Chapter 35 Vacation | Urlaub

Definition, Legal Principles
Every employee in Germany has a legal right to paid vacation. This is regulated by the Federal Paid Leave Act ("Bundesurlaubsgesetz"). The minimum amount of vacation time German law allows is **24 days per annum based on a six-day work week.** Other special vacation regulations arise out of agreements stipulated in individual contract or collective bargaining agreements. Due to these regulations, those working full-time in Germany have an **average of 28–30 vacation days per year.**

The **severely handicapped** have a right to take an additional paid work week off each year. Youth workers also have a right to more vacation time.

Basically, all employment relationships can grant **extra paid leave.** The granting of extra paid leave can be tied to the length of service or certain events, such as the employee's birthday.

Question 470
How many vacation days does an employee working in Germany have per calendar year on average?

Answer
Usually, workers in Germany have **30 vacation days per calendar year.** This correlates to a six-week vacation for a five-day work week. 1

Question 471
How many vacation days per calendar year does German law require employees to have?

Answer
The German Federal Leave Act grants employees in Germany a legal right to **at least 24 work days of vacation.** The rule is based off of a **six-day work week.** There is a **conversion** of the legally provided vacation days on the basis of a five-day work week. In accordance with this, there is a right to 20 work days, in other words four weeks. 2

Example: 3

- 24 working days off for vacation: 6-day work week;
- 20 working days off for vacation: 5-day work week.

Question 472
Is the employee entitled to paid leave beyond his/her vacation entitlement?

Answer
Yes, but entitlement to such leave exists only if the employee is unable to work due to **urgent personal reasons.** The employee retains his/her right to compensation, 4

for example, in case of family events (his/her own wedding, birth of a child, religious celebrations, like a child's first communion, or funerals of close relatives), obligations of honorary office or appointments with public authorities/court dates. In cases of death, the day of the funeral and the days of the death itself will be granted as extra paid leave. If an employee's child becomes ill, that mother or father will be granted up to five days of extra paid leave. For weddings the employee has the option to choose the civil ceremony, church ceremony or both as a two-day block.[1]

Question 473

Does the employer have to pay wages to employees who are on vacation?

Answer

5 The entitlement to vacation time represents the claim to a paid vacation. The amount of the vacation pay is calculated in terms of the average earned income the employee earned during the **thirteen weeks prior to the vacation.**

Question 474

Does the employer have to pay the employee an extra vacation allowance ("Urlaubsgeld")?

Answer

6 No, as **no legal obligation** to pay the employee an extra vacation allowance exists. However, it is often the case that collective bargaining and works agreements provides for this and the payment of vacation allowance is **often observed.**

Question 475

When does an employee gain the right to vacation time?

Answer

7 **A six-month employment relationship** with the given employer within a calendar year is required for a right to the entire legally permitted vacation time. If the employment relationship has been shorter than six months, then there is a claim to a

1 In Germany, a civil ceremony before a registrar of deaths, marriages and births ("Standesbeamter") is required for the marriage to be legally recognized. A church or other religious ceremony is a separate event that the couple may or may not elect to do.

pro-rated vacation time according to sec. 5 of the Federal Paid Leave Act that is reduced by percentages in accordance with the length of the employment relationship. According to this law, the duty of the employer to grant leave should comport with the actual time of employment. Without special rules to the contrary, the employee would not be entitled to vacation time if sec. 5 of the Federal Paid Leave Act were not in force because Article 4 of the same law does not grant the right to full vacation time prior to the employee's sixth month of work. For each month the employment relationship exits, the employee **earns 1/12 of a full-year's vacation allotment**.

Question 476
At what point in the year is the amount of vacation an employee is entitled to determined?

Answer
A vacation year is a **calendar year**. The full annual vacation entitlement occurs on 8
January 1 of a calendar year.

Question 477
Does vacation need to be taken over consecutive days or can it be spread out?

Answer
Vacation time has to be taken over consecutive days unless there is a **work-related** 9
emergency or the particular employee's situation leaves the employer with grounds to make **other arrangements**. If the given vacation taken exceeds twelve work days (for a five-day work week, ten work days) and that vacation time is to be **spread over different time periods**, the specified vacation period has to include at least twelve (or ten) work days.

Question 478
When does the employee have to take vacation?

Answer
The vacation time due has to be taken **during the course of the given calendar** 10
year and may only be taken during the next calendar year in cases of a work-related emergency or the particular employee's situation leaves the employer with reason to make other arrangements. If the vacation due is carried over to the next calendar year, it has to be taken in the **first three months** of that year.

Question 479

When do vacation days expire?

Answer

11 Vacation days expire when they are not taken within a calendar year in which they were accrued or **within the first three months of the following year** into which they were carried over.[2]

Question 480

Do employees have to fill out a vacation request form?

Answer

12 There is no legally mandated formal requirement for vacation requests. A **written request alone serves to provide proof** and should therefore be used for vacation requests.

Question 481

May an employee perform the duties of an honorary office or work elsewhere during a vacation period?

Answer

13 Employment during a vacation is forbidden. The employee may not perform a job that contradicts with the fact that he/she is supposed to be on vacation. Other rules apply only if the **purpose of the vacation is not affected** by the other activity during the vacation period. So, for example, an activity exercised on a regular basis can be performed during a vacation. An honorary office that does not stand in the way of the **employee's relaxation** (the purpose of vacation from a German perspective) does not violate the ban on working during a vacation.

Question 482

What happens if the employee becomes ill during his/her vacation?

Answer

14 If the employee becomes ill during a vacation period, the days that the employee is unable to work due to illness will **not be counted as vacation days**. A **doctor's**

2 See also Question 478.

note that attests that illness would have prevented the employee from working is required. It is immaterial whether the employee can relax despite the illness. The number of days on which the illness prevents the employee from working has to be granted again as vacation to that employee.

Question 483

What happens if, due to a long-term illness, the employee can neither take the vacation due within the given current calendar year nor is able to use the time in the first three months of the following year?

Answer

In cases like this, the claim to the given vacation time does not expire on March 31st of the following year; it expires instead **15 months after the end of the vacation year** in question. 15

Question 484

Once the employee who suffered a long-term illness can work again, what rule(s) apply with respect to his/her vacation time?

Answer

Carried over vacation time of an employee who had been ill for a long time is **subject to the regular guidelines**, which means that the given vacation time has to be taken during that current calendar year and can only be carried over if used by March 31st of the following calendar year. 16

Question 485

Can an employee waive his/her right to vacation time?

Answer

No, waiver of minimum vacation time is not possible. Vacation serving to as a **means of relaxation and recovery** cannot be individually or collectively contractually precluded. Such an agreement is invalid. 17

Question 486

Can the employer shorten someone's vacation time in cases of, for example, illness or pregnancy?

Answer

18 No, the right to vacation days is dependent from the **existence of the employment relationship alone**. The length of time services have been carried out is not important.

Question 487

Can the employer mandate a closure for annual vacation?

Answer

19 Yes, but the employer **has to observe employees' desired dates** for taking their own vacation. The employer can base this closure on his/her wishes and deviate from those of the employees for urgent company concerns.

Question 488

What happens if the employment relationship ends and the employee was unable to take the allowed vacation time beforehand?

Answer

20 In these cases the entitlement to vacation time is **converted into one for compensation**. This entitlement to compensation is a substitute for the vacation time not realized and is **calculated like vacation pay** would be: the average earned income the employee earned during the thirteen weeks prior to the vacation, or, in this case, before the conclusion of the employment relationship.

Question 489

What applies to vacation time that had been carried over from the previous year due to a lengthy illness if the employment relationship ends?

Answer

21 Even carried-over vacation time is converted into an **entitlement to compensation.**

Question 490

What happens to the vacation entitlement if the employment relationship ends because of the death of the employee?

Answer

22 If the employment relationship ends with the employee's death, the vacation entitlement **expires** at that time. It is not converted into an entitlement to compensation for the benefit of the heirs.

Question 491
What special rules apply for teenaged employees?

Answer
German laws considers teens those working who are **15 but are not yet 18.** For this the German Youth Employment Protection Act applies. According to that law, the annual legal entitlement to vacation time is: 23
- at least 30 workdays if the teen is not yet 16 by the beginning of the given calendar year;
- at least 27 work days if the teen is not 17 by the beginning of the given calendar year;
- at least 25 work days if the teen is not yet 18 by the beginning of the given calendar year.
- Teens who work in the mining industry receive additional vacation time of three work days.

Apart from that the fundamental regulations set out in the German Federal Leave Act apply as appropriate. 24

Question 492
What special rules apply for students of vocational schools?

Answer
For adult students of vocational schools the Federal Leave Act regulations apply. 25

Teen students of vocational schools should be given vacation time during the time of their **school break.** So long as there is a school break at the given vocational school, each day attended there during the usual vocational school break earns the teen **an additional day of vacation.** 26

Question 493
Do severely handicapped persons have a right to additional vacation?

Answer
Yes, severely handicapped persons have a right to additional vacation, **five extra days per calendar year.** This does not apply to those who are, for example considered partially handicapped. 27

The entitlement to additional vacation time increases and decreases accordingly if the regular working times of the severely handicapped person are spread over a work week that is more than or less than a five-day calendar work week. If the severely handicapped status is not present for the entire calendar year, the 28 severely handicapped person is entitled to **a twelfth of the extra vacation time for each whole calendar month** he/she is in the employment relationship with severely handicapped status, and fractional amounts of vacation days that amount to at least one-half work day are to be **rounded up to a full day**.

29 If the status of being a severely handicapped person is established **retroactively**, German Employment law regulations establishing grounds for the employment relationship find application for **carrying the extra vacation time over into the next calendar year**.

Chapter 36 Wages | Gehalt

Definition, Legal Principles
Wages represent a sum of money that the employer owes the employee per an employment contract that has been concluded between the two parties. According to the prevailing principle of **freedom of contract** in Germany, the amount wages are set at may be freely agreed upon.

A large number of industry-wide collective agreements in Germany regulate the rates of pay. In addition to wages, employers can offer **special payments**, one very common form being the **bonus**. This is usually a payment that is granted for special occasions (Christmas, vacation or anniversaries marking years of service) and in addition to regular remuneration for work performed. Bonuses are often made at the company's discretion in order to prevent them from gaining the appearance of them becoming a company tradition. Further types of special payments include employer transportation benefits ("Jobtickets"), fitness center coupons, etc.

Question 494
What counts as wages under German law?

Answer
Wages denote remuneration, or the sum for the work that the employer furnishes 1
the employee as a **reward** for the work performed for that employer. This includes compensation in the form of the remuneration and other forms of **monetary payments and non-monetary benefits** (perks).

Question 495
Are the salaries stated in employment contracts denoted as net or gross amounts?

Answer
It is normal in Germany to define the **gross pay** in an employment contract. 2

Question 496
What applies if wages are not agreed upon?

Answer
Under German law wages are considered implicitly agreed upon if there is no dis- 3
cussion about them. That applies for all work performed unless it involves

- the employee accommodating the employer at the last-minute,
- volunteer work, or
- informal assistance.

Question 497
Does Germany have a minimum wage?

Answer
4 Currently, there is no unified, legally recognized minimum wage in Germany. However, there are **certain sectors** where rules on a minimum wage apply. Included is the posting of employees with the following industries:
- construction,
- commercial cleaning,
- mail delivery,
- laundry and security services,
- specialized mining work,
- waste management, and
- certain educational and training services.

Question 498
Is there a cap on wages?

Answer
5 No, there is no cap on wages in Germany.

Question 499
Which allowances and additional pay does the employer have to pay for?

Answer
6 The paying of additional compensation and allowances is largely a **subject of collective bargaining and individual contracts**. To the point, they will be paid for work performed under circumstances that are **especially hard** or that are **life-threatening** (hardship allowance – “Erschwerniszulage”). Other additional compensation comes in the form of overnight and alternating shift pay, social security allowances, performance bonuses, or additional pay for working on Sundays or holidays.

Question 500
What does the employer have to pay for extra work or overtime?

Answer
7 There is no special law regarding the compensation of extra work or overtime. From collective bargaining agreements and individual contracts, the employee

is entitled to compensation for overtime by way of monetary pay or time off. The **employer determines the type of compensation.** If there is no contractual stipulation, compensation in line with the usual hourly wage is implicitly agreed upon.

Question 501
Is vacation money required to be paid out in Germany?

Answer
No. Vacation pay is a **lump sum payment** above the regular paid leave the em- 8
ployee may be entitled to. It is a **special payment from the employer**, and he/she is only obligated to make such payment if a special legal basis exists for it, such as by way of an individual employment contract. An employer have the right to stipulate in an employment contract whether or not vacation money would be decided upon on a year-to-year basis or if it should be made at all.

Question 502
In Germany, does Christmas bonus need to be paid out to employees?

Answer
No. Payment of Christmas bonus ("Weihnachtsgeld") is an extra payment made by 9
employers along with regular wages. It is made on a **voluntary basis**, and there is no legal right to one, with the exception of civil servants. However, an employer may not arbitrarily decide to pay one employee a Christmas bonus and not others. It is further important for employers to be aware that the repeated payment of a Christmas bonus represents to the employee a **company-wide tradition** that the employer would be obligated to pay again in future years. Moreover, Christmas bonuses cannot be arbitrarily discontinued.

Question 503
Is there a requirement in Germany for the payment of long-service anniversary bonuses?

Answer
Bonuses for length of service and loyalty bonuses represent **extra payments** that 10
reward a certain period of employment with a given company. Like Christmas bonuses and vacation pay, bonuses for length of service are bonuses that **may be paid out** but do not have to be.

Question 504
Is variable compensation usual in Germany?

Answer
11 Performance-oriented payment is becoming **more and more common** in Germany. Thus, the employee's motivation and readiness to work should increase and drops in profit will be absorbed. Often variable compensation can be found in **service companies** with executives and management positions. The portion of the variable compensation varies in each sector and increases as one reaches a higher position in a given company.

Question 505
What types of variable compensation are there in Germany?

Answer
12 Variable compensation is usually based on a **profit-sharing model.** In this case it is calculated according to company profit or an increase in the value of the company. Variable compensation can also be geared to the **individual performance** of the given employee or to **customer satisfaction** based on his or her performance. Variable compensation is paid out via bonuses, equity warrants or profit-sharing.

Question 506
Can the employer reduce an employee's wages?

Answer
13 Job performance and compensation for it stand in a balanced relation to one another. That means that wages **may not be reduced arbitrarily**. Such a ban on arbitrary wage reduction bears comparison to when the employer demands more work from the employee for the same pay.

14 On the other hand, if an **employee's work is delayed** by the action or inaction of the employer (e.g. telling the employee there is no work for that day, the machines are out of order, the employer is out of raw materials, etc.), it cannot be made up later by the employee (German concept of fixed obligation of work performance – "Fixschuldcharakter"), and, the employer is not authorized to reduce one's wages in such instances, either. However, the employer remains legally **obligated to compensate.**

15 The obligation of the employer to pay wages also continues in cases of illness, holidays, and vacation time. If the employee is released from working, the obligation of the employer to pay is determined in the same manner in accordance with legal provisions.

Question 507
When does the employer have to pay wages?

Answer
The employer's obligation to pay wages arises when the **claim to payment becomes due**. That said, the employee has an obligation to perform the given work prior to compensation. That means that the claim for pay first becomes due **after the employee has completed the work** he/she is supposed to do. If the compensation is measured in periods of time, it is to be paid at the conclusion of that period according to German law. Something else might be agreed on in an employment contract. 16

Question 508
What happens if the employer fails to pay wages?

Answer
By not paying wages, the employer is **violating his/her primary obligation** to the employee. According to German law, the employee can use the German courts to enforce this right to payment of wages with an action for performance or **assert a claim for damages** from the employer. In this context, the employee's rights do not survive, so long as the employer legitimately pays back the part of the wages that may be legally seized, or sets off the claims vis-à-vis the employee. 17

Question 509
What happens if the employer pays out wages late?

Answer
An employer allowing payday to pass without compensating his/her employees represents a **breach of duty**. With such a failure, the employer defaults on debts and then **becomes liable for damages**. 18

With considerable wages in arrears over a **longer period of time**, the employee receives a right to **withhold his/her work until counter-performance** (i.e. compensation) is effected, which means the employee can refuse to do work the employer asks for with a view to the latter's breach of duty. 19

Question 510
What does the employer have to pay beyond wages?

Answer

20 The employer has the **obligation of withholding and paying income tax**. Further, the employer has the obligation to adhere to social security regulations as stated in the German Social Security Code ("Sozialgesetzbuch"), thereby not infringing the employee's rights related to social security. He/she also has to register the employee and **pay the required contributions** to statutory retirement, health, compulsory long-term care, unemployment, and casualty insurances.

21 The employee whose pay exceeds the **limit for mandatory insurance** in the statutory health insurance system is freed from paying into that system, but the employer still has to pay a contribution for that employee's health insurance, as it is a **debt liability** ("Haftungsschuld").

Question 511

What happens if the employer fails to make these contributions?

Answer

22 The employer has a debt liability for income tax and social security contributions. If the employer does not pay these contributions in a proper fashion, he/she could incur a penalty under German law and is obligated to **refund the remaining payments**.

Question 512

Does an employer have to keep a payroll account?

Answer

23 Yes, according to German law, the employer has to keep a payroll account for its employees at work establishment/work-site.

Question 513

Does the employer have to keep payroll records?

Answer

24 Payroll records include information about the accounting period, the gross pay, deductions from net wages and serve as a **basis for bookkeeping's calculations**. The employer has to keep such payroll records as a part of the payroll account.

Question 514

What rights of inspection does the works council have?

Answer

The works council has the responsibility of seeing that employee-friendly regulations are followed. In fact, they enjoy a **right to information** in those areas where regulations affecting employees exist so that the works council can meet this obligation. In personnel matters the works council has a **right to inspect the records** the company required to keep for works council decisions about hiring, job classification or reclassification and transfer. An **inspection of personnel files** is permitted upon by request of the given employee. 25

Question 515

Does the employer have to make advanced wage payments?

Answer

In otherwise unrecoverable employee emergency financial situations – e.g. severe illness or death – there is an obligation to make advance payment, which, under German Law, is derived primarily from the employer's **obligation of employee welfare** and, as a secondary obligation, from the employment relationship. 26

Aside from emergency cases, the employer does not have to make advanced wage payments. The employee has an obligation to perform the given work prior to compensation. Yet, the employer can contractually agree upon advanced payments with the employee on an **individual basis**. Advance payment made will be offset on the next payday by the work performed in the next paycheck. 27

Question 516

Does the employer have to assume the employee's moving costs?

Answer

There is an obligation to pay moving costs if the employee has been **relocated for business reasons**. Thus, the move has to be necessary for operational reasons. Commuting must be too much to expect from the employee. However, the reimbursement of moving costs can be **coupled with the time commitment to the company**. An earlier exit of the employee (i.e. by retirement or leaving the firm) leads to an obligation to reimburse moving costs. 28

For **moves for reasons** other than those which are **company-related**, the employer does not have to reimburse the employee for moving costs. However, terms of individual, works or collective bargaining agreements can deviate from this. 29

Question 517

Does the employer have to pay into capital-building payment/state-supported savings plans?

Answer

30 If there is no individual contract, the employer is only obligated to pay contributions for state-supported saving plans when stipulated in the collective bargaining or works agreement. The **collective bargaining agreements** with respect to this matter include the metal, electrical, chemical industries and those industries that manufacture lumber and plastics, as well as public service.

Question 518

Does the employer have to convert wages into pension plan at the employee's request?

Answer

31 The employer can request that a portion of his/her wages be used for a pension plan, the so-called "deferred compensation plan" in German Law ("Entgeltumwandlung"). **Up to 4%** of the social security contribution ceiling ("Beitragsbemessungsgrenze") from future compensation claims for the regular pension can be used for the company pension plan by way of wage conversion at the request of the employee. The condition is that it **involves pension, invalidity, and survivor's benefits.** If this is not the case, the provision represents an employee personal insurance plan.

Question 519

Does the employer have to pay travelling expenses?

Answer

32 Travel to work is to be included in the personal sphere of the employee. There is no legal obligation of the employer in Germany to cover such costs. Other rules apply for incidental **business-related travel** so long as that travel is not covered in the employee's pay.

Question 520

Does the employer have to pay for or provide the employee with work clothes?

Answer

33 According to German law, the employer is obligated to **make protective clothing available** to his/her employees so long as this is necessary to protect the "life

and limbs" of the employee. If there is such an obligation to provide protective clothing, the employee has a claim for reimbursement to the extent that he/she may deem necessary for attaining the clothing him/herself. Beyond this, there are **no additional claims** for reimbursement of work clothing expenses under German law.

Question 521

What other things of monetary value does the employer have to pay for?

Answer

If the employee uses his own assets in the interest of the employer without being 34
compensated for doing so, that employee has a **claim to be reimbursed** by the employer. Expenses incurred for things that the employer did not request or work not required does not need to be compensated by the employer. This would include lifestyle expenses, such usage of luxury cars or gym memberships.

In addition to that there can be other reasons, ones based on individual or col- 35
lective agreements, that obligate the employer to **provide for things of monetary value**. For example, there is a right of survivors of federal employees to claim for a funeral allowance.

Question 522

Does the employer have to pay for the employee's discoveries?

Answer

Yes, the employer has to pay for the discovery so long as it was completed during 36
the time of the employment relationship. This applies, however, only to discoveries and technical improvements that are **patentable or capable of protection as a utility model**. Obligation to pay exists with an expressly declared or fictitious use. The employee does not have to wait for a protective-right application procedure. Yet, the employer can **withhold a partial payment** until the final decision from the German Patent and Trademark Office because of the risk of granting shared property rights ("Schutzrechtserteilungsrisiko"). Refusal of the patent application can only have affects for the future application of the discovery. Monies already paid to the employee cannot be demanded back.

Question 523

Does the employer have to provide loans to employees?

Answer

37 No, employers have **no obligation to provide loans** to their employees. Supported by a loan agreement between employer and employee, the loan represents a company wage policy and is subject to the co-determination of staff representatives.

Chapter 37 Working Hours | Arbeitszeit

Definition, Legal Principles

!

Working Hours in Germany are regulated by the German Working Hours Act ("Arbeitszeitrecht"), which addresses **different regulatory subject matters**, including the establishment of boundaries within which those setting contractual working hours rules can operate. What is specifically set is the maximum working hours, length of breaks and rest periods and regulations regarding the timeframes for work, including work on Sundays and holidays.

The purpose of law protecting working times and above all the German Working Hours Act itself is to guaranty the **health and safety for employees** in the organization with reasonable working times and to improve the general conditions for flexible working times. The maximum number of hours allowed to be worked is regulated by the Working Hours Act and some other protective acts governed by public law.

The weekly amount of hours to be worked is found in **collective bargaining agreements** and **individual employment agreements**. These agreements also determine what working times will be considered compensated and whether the employee has to work overtime. Daily working times and hours to be worked are determined by the employer per his/her supervisory authority over employees.

But, employers have to observe the participatory rights held by the works council in this context. The works council has **co-determination rights** regarding the time for the beginning and end of the working day, as well as breaks and overtime or temporary reduction of working hours.

Question 524

What is generally included in the working hour regulations?

Answer

To differentiate, there are three areas: 1

- the German Working Hours Act,
- the contractual working hour regulations, and
- the working hour regulations related to co-determination rights.

The rules regarding German working-hours regulations, especially the Working Hours Act ("Arbeitszeitgesetz"), standardize binding general legal requirements for employee **working hours**. The contractual working hour regulations determine during which **time periods the employee has to produce or perform his/her work**, as well as what **claim he/she has to compensation** pursuant to agreements. The working hour regulations related to co-determination rights regulate the scope of employee rights of participation that the works council has according to the German Works Constitution Act ("Betriebsverfassungsgesetz"). 2

Question 525

How long may an employee in Germany work and how are weekly working hours arranged in Germany?

Answer

3 The legally permitted **maximum working hours** for an employee is **eight hours per workday**. Workdays include all days of the week except for Sunday and legal holidays, which may vary from state to state in Germany. The Working Hours Act is based on a six-day-week and **weekly working hours totaling 48 hours**. The daily working hours can be **extended to ten hours** if it is within six calendar months or within 24 weeks, and an average of eight hours per day will not be exceeded.

Question 526

What is the difference between overtime and excess hours worked?

Answer

4 German Federal Labor Court speaks of "overtime compensated with time in lieu" (i.e. flextime) or "paid overtime" if the **agreed upon working hours for the particular employment relationship** are exceeded, which would be those set by collective or individual agreement.

5 "Excess hours worked" are understood as those extra hours worked that exceed the **legally permissible maximum working hours**.

Question 527

Does an employee have to work overtime hours?

Answer

6 There is no legal obligation. Overtime is only to be worked in extraordinary circumstances i.e. emergencies. However, the employee and employer can adjust the employment contract so that the employee has to work overtime. If this is the case, the employer is **authorized to instruct** the employee at any time to work overtime **without extra notification**.

Question 528

What happens if the employee does not work the permissibly mandated overtime hours?

Answer

7 If the employee refuses to perform permissibly mandated overtime hours, **terminating the employment relationship is justifiable**. That said, the employee has to have been warned beforehand.

Question 529

Does the employer have to compensate for overtime worked by a salaried employee?

Answer

There is no legal rule to pay extra compensation for automatic overtime or each instance of presence for work that is above the agreed-upon or typical working hours for a said company. If there is no rule about compensation in the employment contract, the issue of whether or not there is an obligation to compensate for overtime exists **needs to be determined**. It has to involve **mandated or authorized overtime**. Case law requires a particularly **higher amount of work from highly paid employees**, even if the typical working hours of a given company is exceeded by working those extra hours. 8

Question 530

Can overtime be compensated by a lump-sum payment?

Answer

There is a **20% rule** with average wages. That means that up to **eight overtime hours a week based on a 40-hour working week** would count as compensated with such a payment. 9

Question 531

Does the employer have to compensate for overtime worked by an hourly-wage employee?

Answer

With hourly wages, compensation for overtime with the basic rate of pay goes without question. The agreement of a monthly wage being simultaneously set for when the amount of the working time is, justifies the conclusion that the agreement applies to monthly compensation for the work performed by the employee within the agreed-upon time period. Further, overtime has to be paid based on the **portion of the monthly salary that corresponds to one hour of work.** 10

Question 532

May an employee work at night?

Answer

Yes, the permissibility of working night hours is based on the German Working Hours Act. The working times of employees working at night is further determined 11 according to the verified ergonomic studies' findings about work to be adequately designed for humans. For employees working at night the principle of eight-hour workdays with the possibility of extending to ten hours applies, but with a **shorter comp time period** from a calendar month or of four weeks. Employees working at night are **entitled to have themselves medically examined** before beginning working these hours and in regular intervals after that point.

Question 533
What models for working times are there?

Answer
12 There are
- time-credit accounts,
- flextime systems, and
- working time based on an honors system.

Question 534
How do time-credit accounts ("Arbeitszeitkonten") in Germany work?

Answer
13 With the general term time-credit account, a wide range of different models for increased flexibility of working times are understood. There are **two basic types** that are common:
- annual-hours contracts, and
- set-aside accounts.

Question 535
What is an annual-hours contract?

Answer
14 On the basis of annual-hours contracts, the employment contract can determine a set volume of work to be spread over an annual planning period instead of a weekly or monthly one. That way it is possible **to plan flexibly foreseeably long-term**, but intermittent working needs within a **one-year period**.

Question 536
How does a set-aside account work in Germany?

Answer

Set-aside accounts open the opportunity to the employee **to save hours worked** 15
above regular work hours for a transition period outside of his/her regular work life, despite the continuation of the employment relationship. The account may be used for things such as extended vacation time, continuing education or training or early partial or full retirement, and the employee still receives his/her full salary.

Question 537

How does flextime work in Germany?

Answer

Only during a **particular, set core working time** does an attendance requirement 16
exist for the employee. Besides this, the employee can freely use his/her time outside of the time period during which the flextime is to be worked.

Question 538

What is meant by working hours based on an honors system?

Answer

The employer foregoes recording time worked and other forms of direct checks on 17
working time. Time management and attendance at the workplace are stipulated at the **discretion of the employee**. Individual targets are defined work results and objectives.

Question 539

What rest periods in work does the employee have to take?

Answer

Rest periods for the employee are set by statute. For working periods of six to nine 18
hours, there must be a 30-minute rest period; for working periods above nine hours there must be a 45-minute break. A break must be **at least 15 minutes**, otherwise it counts as working time. The Working Hours Act does not define the term break. According to German Federal Labor Court, this deals with a pre-planned break in work in which the employee can freely decide where and how he or she will spend this time. The employee has **to be exempted from having to perform work** of any kind during such breaks.

Question 540

May work take place on Sundays and government holidays?

Answer

19 Generally not. The making employees work on Sundays and government holidays is **forbidden for all areas of employment**. This is a result of the constitutional requirement of Sunday being a day of rest ("Sonntagsruhe") and that the statutory holiday rest periods be observed. The ban on employees working on Sundays and government holidays is **not dispositive**. Individual or collective agreements, which contravene this work ban are null and void. However, the German Working Hours Act includes a comprehensive catalog of areas in which employees may work on Sundays or government holidays so long as the work cannot be performed on a traditional workday.

Question 541

Which statutory rest times does the employee have to take?

Answer

20 For the employee an **uninterrupted rest period of at least eleven hours** after the end of daily working hours is to be observed. Working Hours Act does not provide a legal definition of rest period. A rest period means, however, that the period of time between the end of daily working hours and the start of the next period of daily working hours.

Question 542

Is travel to work (travel time) work time?

Answer

21 No, it is not. The time that the employee spends traveling to and from work is in the **private sphere** and therefore associated with a rest period. Travel time for travel from the place of business to and from an off-site place of business is counted as regular working hours. The same can apply for both ways of travel for business trips.

Question 543

What is meant by Germans with "readiness to work" ("Arbeitsbereitschaft")?

Answer

22 "Readiness to work" is defined by the German Federal Labor Court as a **sort of work** that does not entirely engage the employee, and thus **does not require his/her full**

attention. Some examples include taxi or limo drivers who are waiting to take a client somewhere or a fire fighter who is awaiting a call to duty. Here, the employer has sent the employee to work, and the employee, though awake, can relax, for being ready to work represents a minimal performance of work compared to full performance of work.

Readiness to work has to be distinguished from rest period. In the latter, the employee is **not obligated to keep him/herself in a constant state of wakeful attentiveness** to commence work. 23

Question 544
What is meant by on stand-by work?

Answer
This is the time period during which the employee has to **stay in a particular place** 24
within or outside of the place of business for business reasons. In this manner the employee can start working as needed, be that immediately or promptly. To be on stand-by is not the full performance of work, but instead a limitation on where the employee can be (how far from the place of work, for example); and this comes with the obligation to **commence work without delay when needed**. Stand-by work counts as working hours.

Question 545
How counts as being on-call in Germany?

Answer
Being on-call obligates the employee to **commence work when phoned**. In com- 25
parison to stand-by work, the employee can remain at a place of his/her choice that the employer is aware of. The employee has to ensure that he/she may be **reached at any time**. Being on-call counts towards the employee's working hours.

Question 546
What counts as shift work?

Answer
Shift work is not statutorily regulated. According to the Federal Labor Court, how- 26
ever, shift work exists if the work task is completed as an employee's daily work over an extended period and **performed by several employees in a set chronological order**. For shift work the general provisions of working hours applies. Shift work can be introduced into **all sectors of business**. The German Working Hours

Act contains an opening clause for collective agreements. Beyond that the Working Hours Act does not have special regulations. So long as the employee works both day and night shifts, the regulations for working at night apply.

Question 547

Does the employer have an obligation to report?

Answer

27 Yes, the employer is **obligated to make a copy** of the Federal Working Hours Act visible for inspection in suitable workplace areas or to give employees copies.

Question 548

Does the employer have an obligation to keep records?

Answer

28 Yes, the employer has to keep records about hours worked that surpass those on normal work days (i.e. overtime). Not covered here are **working hours of up to eight hours on workdays** (Monday to Saturday).

Chapter 38 Works Agreement | Betriebsvereinbarung

Definition, Legal Principles

!

Under German law, works agreements represent the legal instrument that is available to employees and employers to reach agreements that work within the legal framework and which is **compulsory** and goes **into force with immediate effect**. They can be limited in time and be terminated. Further, they have to be in writing and require the signature of both parties. With respect to content, a works agreement can regulate all questions where the works council has **co-determination rights**.

A difference must be made here, however, between a **mandatory** works agreement and a **voluntary** works agreement. A works agreement is mandatory if the law determines an arrangement cannot be reached without works council input. A more frequent application mandatory works agreements is with respect to co-determination (aka "participatory") rights for social matters found in sec. 87 of the German Works Agreement Act ("Betriebsverfassungsgesetz – BetrVG"). If no agreement is arrived at in cases where mandatory co-determination rights are at question, the decision of a **conciliation board** replaces the agreement and operates as a works agreement.

On the other hand, if the given situation is about stipulations that are already defined by law or the collective agreement, or that is normally regulated by a collective bargaining agreement, it cannot be part of a works agreement. Example: stipulations regarding wages or weekly working times.

Question 549

What is a works agreement?

Answer

There is no legal standard for a works agreement. According to the German Federal Labor Court, it is a **written contract** between an employer and a works council that is concluded to set legal norms. It establishes the rights and responsibilities of the parties and formulates **binding standards for all company employees**. 1

Question 550

What is an internal agreement ("Regelungsabrede")?

Answer

An internal agreement is an **in personam contract**. It does not have standardizing effects comparable to a works agreement. An internal agreement does not require a particular form. That said, it has to be in writing in order to provide evidence of the agreement. 2

Question 551

To whom does a works agreement apply?

Answer

3 A works agreement applies to **all company employees**. Under German law, an employee is any person who has an employer-employee relationship to the employer. The works agreement applies to both those who are currently employed as well as those who are hired after the agreement goes into effect.

Question 552

To whom does a works agreement not apply?

Answer

4 Works agreements do not apply to and are invalid for **upper management/executives.**

Question 553

Can a works agreement be agreed upon for specific groups of employees?

Answer

5 Yes, but there needs to be a clear rule in the works agreement and the clear designation of the affected employee group. Taking **non-discrimination principles** into consideration, the scope of a works agreement can be limited to specific departments (e.g. administration) or specific employee groups (e.g. sales reps).

Question 554

How do works agreements come about?

Answer

6 They come about **via resolution.**

Question 555

Who concludes a works agreement?

Answer

7 The employer and the works council conclude the works agreement jointly. For a joint resolution there has to be **two corresponding letters of intent** with regard to the entire content of the concluded works agreement.

Question 556
What can be in the content of a works agreement?

Answer
A works agreement can contain the **agreement of the resolution** and the **ending** 8
of the agreement. It can also show company or works council constitution law agreements.

Question 557
What may not be in the content of a works agreement?

Answer
Employees' daily life outside of the workplace may not be included in a works 9
agreement.

Question 558
Does a works agreement have to be in writing?

Answer
Yes, it is required that a works agreement is in written form, and it has to be **signed** 10
by the employer and works council in order to be valid. The signatures have to be on the document. The exchange of documents signed by one party is legally insufficient.

Question 559
Does a works agreement have to be made public?

Answer
The works agreement has to be **displayed in an appropriate, accessible place** at 11
the company. For example, an appropriate place would be one where employees can take notice of the works agreement without difficulty (i.e. a break room). It would also legally suffice if the publication is in **electronic format**, e.g. Intranet.

Question 560
Who has to display the works agreement?

Answer
The employer has to display the works agreement. 12

Question 561
What are the consequences for the employer if that employer does not display the works agreement?

Answer
13 There is no liability for damages. However, there can be **penalties** levied against the employer for not displaying the document.

Question 562
Geographically speaking, where does a works agreement apply?

Answer
14 A works agreement applies at the **particular establishment** for which it was concluded.

Question 563
Does a works agreement apply to the entire company if there are several sites?

Answer
15 Yes, so long as the works agreement does specifically stipulate otherwise.

Question 564
Upon whom is it incumbent to execute the works agreement?

Answer
16 The employer has the duty to **execute the agreement**. Note, however, that German law allows for transferring the responsibility to the works council.

Question 565
How does a works agreement end?

Answer
17 It ends with the **lapse of time** if there has been a fixed term agreed upon.

Question 566
How long is it before a typical works agreement expires?

Answer

There is no law regarding the length of time before a works agreement expires. The length of time before it expires can be **freely agreed upon** by the employer and works council. 18

Question 567

Can a works agreement also be terminated?

Answer

Yes, it is possible to terminate a works agreement. 19

Question 568

How long is the notice period for terminating a works agreement?

Answer

The works agreement can be terminated with a **three-month notice period** if there are no special regulations hindering that from happening. 20

Question 569

Can a works agreement be contested?

Answer

Yes, if there is a reason for contesting the works agreement. Reasons considered valid for contesting the works agreement include error, fraudulent misrepresentation, and threats. The works agreement's legal force **ends with future effect** and does not retroactively apply. 21

Question 570

Is the works agreement terminated if there is a transfer of business?

Answer

No, the works agreement **remains valid** in case of a surviving business identity. 22

Question 571

Is the entire works agreement invalid if parts of it are?

Answer

23 What is crucial here is whether the valid parts of the works agreement still **contain sensible regulations** without the invalid parts. If this is the case, the remainder of the works agreement is valid.

Question 572

What is the relationship of a works agreement to a collective bargaining agreement with a union?

Answer

24 Both documents exist side by side. A works council agreement supersedes only those individual contractual stipulations that **do not work in the employee's favor**, the principle of deviation for employee´s benefit from the collective bargaining agreement ("Günstigkeitsprinzip").

Question 573

Is a works agreement subject to examination by a German labor court?

Answer

25 Yes, the works agreement has to **comply with law and equity**.

Question 574

Are there special income tax law features that need to be observed?

Answer

26 Not with works agreements. The benefits that the employee receives from the works agreement are to be assessed in accordance with **income tax law criteria**.

Chapter 39 Works Council | Betriebsrat

Definition, Legal Principles
A works council is the co-determination (participatory) body for the workforce of a company that represents the interests of employees involving the employer for companies with **at least five permanent employees.** German law does not require the establishment of a works council; it is up to the employees, but they are common. Forty-five percent of all workers in the western German states private sector employees are represented by a works council; about 38% of those working in the five eastern German states share the same sort of representation.[1]

The works council's functions, rights and obligations are stipulated by the Works Constitution Act ("Betriebsverfassungsgesetz – BetrVG"). In certain sectors it has **varying rights of audience, consultation and co-determination.** The works council members are elected to four-year terms, with its actual establishment as a functioning body taking place after its elections. The size of a works council is determined by number of employee in accordance with sec. 9 of the Works Constitution Act.

One important operational point to keep in mind is that works council members are to be **released from regular work duties without reduction in pay** so long as it is necessary for their works council duties according to the nature and scale of operations.

I. General Aspects

Question 575
What is a works council?

Answer
A works council is an elected, co-determination body of employees that plays a con- 1
siderable role in governing labor relations. It is **representative of the personnel.** But, it is not representative of particular employee groups, especially not unions and their membership. It does not represent executives. They are represented by a spokesperson for company officers.

Question 576
Is there an obligation to establish a works council?

Answer
No, there is no obligation on the part of either the employee, union or employer to 2
establish a works council.

1 Status as of 2009, see Hans Böckler Foundation (http://www.boeckler.de).

Question 577

Can the creation of a works council be prevented?

Answer

3 No, German law prohibits and makes **punishable negotiations** that hinder the election or a works council or the carrying out of its work.

Question 578

Can a works council be dissolved?

Answer

4 Yes, but the dissolution of a works council requires an **organizational breach of duty** on their part and, taking into account all circumstances of the individual cases, a determination must be made that continuing to carry out the offices of the works council would be determined. Dissolution might take place, for example, in the following circumstances: with a resolution for an illegal job action, with uncivil or repeated violations of promoting a political party on company grounds, or by virtue of not appointing a works council chairperson or vice-chairperson.

Question 579

Who is in the works council?

Answer

5 The works council is composed of employees of the given company. All who have been employed at the company **for at least six months** may vote for or be elected to the works council. If the company is under six-months old, employees who were **involved in initiating the works council election** at the place or work may be elected.

Question 580

Can a works council member be fired?

Answer

6 A works council member has **special protection from dismissal** due to his/her works council membership. In instances of ordinary dismissal, this applies for the duration of the works council term in office plus one year that follows that term. A **summary dismissal** from the job would require the permission of the works council.

Question 581

How large are works councils?

Answer

The size of a works council is **determined by the number of employees** at the company in question. For example: 7

- the works council at a company of 5–20 employees consists of one person;
- in organizations with 21–50 employees, the works council would be three people;
- in companies with 51–100 employees, the works council would be five people; and,
- with a company of 101–200 employees, the works council would be seven people.

In other words, the number of works council members **increases with the number of employees.** 8

Question 582

Can the stipulated size of the works council be deviated from?

Answer

No, the allocation of works council size in relation to the number of employees is **compulsory**. It cannot be deviated from. Only exceptions arising out of the German Works Constitution Act itself are considered. This would be the case at a company without a sufficient number of employees, one which would work off of the basis of the **number of works council members at the next smallest-sized company**. 9

Question 583

At what point does the employer have to release a works council member for the completion of his/her works council duties?

Answer

The works council has the legal right to release one works council member in companies of 200 or more employees for works council work, more than twelve members would be released in companies of over 10.000. Works council members in companies of under 200 employees are to be **freed from the work duties if it is necessary**. A necessity exits if the works council member considers his or her absence from working in order complete works council duties to be **essential**. Being freed from performing his or her job does not require the permission of the employer. The works council member nevertheless **has to inform the employer**. 10

Question 584
Does an employer need to be notified by a works council member of that employee's performance of works council duties?

Answer
11 Yes, the works council member has to inform the employer of works council duties so that the company can carry out the **necessary operational changes** due to the works council member's absence.

Question 585
How long is the typical term of office for works council members?

Answer
12 The term of a works council members is statutorily stipulated to be **four years**. The term begins with the announcement of the election results and ends with the end of the period in office.

Question 586
What exceptions are there?

Answer
13 Beyond the regular term of four years, a need for new elections may arise if, **within a period of 24 months**:
- the number of employees drops or increases by roughly half,
- the number of works council members has dropped to a number below the statutory minimum number of members after several replacement members have stood in,
- when the given works council has decided to resign based on a majority vote of members,
- the works council election results are successfully contested,
- the works council is dissolved,
- there is no existing works council at the given company.

Question 587
Which positions are there in a larger works council?

Answer
14 Every larger works council has to elect a works council **chairperson** and a **vice-chairperson.**

Question 588
What are the duties of the works council chairperson?

Answer
The works council chairperson **opens, leads and closes works council meetings.** 15
He/she declares the results of the collective decisions and sets the rules during meetings. The works council chairperson may give the floor or take it back as he/she sees fit. That said, the chairperson must **exercise house rules** in the meeting room(s). He/she leads the works meeting. He/she is an ex-officio member of the works committee and authorized to take part in meetings and consultation hours with youth and trainee representatives. Beyond this it is incumbent upon the works council chairperson to take on the **external representation** of the works council, for example, within the context of agreed upon decisions. He/she does not have the right to make decisions on his own.

Question 589
What are the duties of the vice-chairperson?

Answer
The vice-chairperson **does not have any of his own functions** besides acting 16
works council chairperson. He or she represents the works council in cases of the chairperson's absence or when the chairperson is personally affected by the issue at hand, for example by a hearing on his own prospective dismissal.

Question 590
How does the works council arrive at its decisions?

Answer
It arrives at its decisions by way of **resolutions.** 17

Question 591
How is a works council meeting run?

Answer
Led by the works council chairperson, works council meetings are **not public.** Min- 18
utes of the meeting are taken and must contain the wording of prepared resolutions and the majority vote. The minutes are to be signed by the works council chairperson and one additional member and an attendance list is to be attached to the minutes. On this list, those present must **sign by hand.**

Question 592
Which committees does the works council have to form?

Answer
19 Works councils with nine or more members have to establish a committee. The works committee is a part of the works council. Its **main function is leading the current business** of the works council. The establishment of other committees is not required. In companies of over 100 employees the works council can establish further committees that can be given specific duties. In addition to this, the works council and the employer can also set up a **joint committee**. In order to fulfill practical needs the works council can also establish **working groups** in order to complete specific tasks.

Question 593
Can individual works council members be barred from the works council?

Answer
20 If individual or all works council members commit a **breach of duty** in parallel that is not based on a joint resolution of the works council, proceedings to bar a member(s) may take place – not the dissolution of the entire works council per se.

Question 594
What company resources does the employer need to provide the works council?

Answer
21 The employer is obligated to make office materials, equipment, rooms and office personnel available to the works council **as required**. Some examples of office materials and equipment include the usual things found in an office, such as information and communication technology like a computer with an internet connection and a telephone with a working line. The required literature is also to be made available. In short, so long as the works council needs office personnel to perform their work, the employer must provide that help.

Question 595
Who covers the cost for the works council and what do these costs consist of?

Answer
22 Works council costs are **covered by the employer**. The costs stem from those from the current works council management. Those costs relates those for

- materials, equipment, and office personnel,
- costs for usage of an interpreter, an expert, or a written translation,
- the costs of the works council election,
- the required costs of labor court proceedings or other legal disputes,
- costs incurred by individual works council members for works council business, which would include travel costs and those for arbitration.

Question 596
Does the employer have to pay for works council trainings?

Answer
Only if the training is necessary. There is necessity if the training is in consideration 23
of the **clear relation to the company's needs** and those of the works council, so that the work council can complete its current work in the near future and in a proper and professional manner. Mere usefulness does not suffice. There has to be a **clear link to company matters**, and one exists if the training is suitable for conveying professional knowledge to employees.

Question 597
Do trainings constitute working hours?

Answer
Yes, required trainings count as working hours. If the training takes place outside of 24
regular working hours, the works council member is entitled to **additional compensation.**

Question 598
May the works council hire consultants?

Answer
Yes, the works council **has the option** of using an external consultant for carrying 25
out its work. Consultants are people who give the works council **advice they lack that is of a professional or legal nature**. This serves to properly fulfill tasks in cooperation with the employer. The consultant is subject to **duty of professional confidentiality**. The consultant does not have to remain neutral in his or her role as consultant; the works council can in fact support the exercising of its interests with the consultant's expertise. The conditions for using an outside consultant is based on the necessity of the involvement. This is, for example, given when consulting attorneys about difficult legal questions.

Question 599
Who covers the costs for the contracting of consultants?

Answer
26 Works council costs are covered by the employer.

Question 600
Does the employer have to allow works council members time away from work for their works council duties?

Answer
27 Yes, works council members are **to be made temporarily available for concrete works council purposes.** A concrete purpose would be if the time away from work served the perception of works council duties. With conscientious consideration and reasonable acknowledgment of all circumstances of the particular situation, the time away from work **has to be necessary** from the view of the affected works council member. It also **has to be urgent**. The agreement of the employer is not necessary.

Question 601
What applies with regard to compensation of a works council member given leave for his works council duties?

Answer
28 With time off of work for such duties, the works council member is to continue receiving the **same level of compensation** received when working his or her regular job. What does not have to be compensated is the employer's work that counts as compensation for expenses, such as those for travel. Actually, such costs are not generated by the works council member.

Question 602
What is a representative committee of executive employees ("Sprecherausschuss")?

Answer
29 A representative committee of executive employees **represents the interests of executive staff** in plant or company. It corresponds to the works council. The representative committee of executive employees is only **entitled to informational and consultation rights**. Representative committees of executive employees can be elected in the company in which there are **at least ten executive-level employees** regularly working.

II. Election of the Works Council Members

Question 603
How is the works council elected?

Answer
The election takes place in a **constituent meeting** of the works council. Election regulations control the holding of the election. Those regulations include the works council being voted upon in a **secret and direct election.** A proportional election counts. Employees with the right to vote and unions can make nominations. 30

Question 604
Can the works council election be contested by the employer?

Answer
Yes, it can be contested if voting regulations, eligibility requirements, or the electoral procedure have been **significantly violated** and the requisite **reporting did not follow the given election.** An exception would exist where the election results would not have been changed or influenced. 31

Question 605
Who else is entitled to contest the outcome?

Answer
At least three employees who are entitled to vote, one who is in the union to which the employees belong or the employer may contest the outcome. 32

Question 606
Until what point can the results of a works council election be contested?

Answer
The election results can be contested up until **two weeks** after the date that the results are made public. 33

Question 607
Who is responsible for handling a challenge to the election results?

Answer

34 The **labor court** is responsible in such instances.

Question 608

When is a works council election void?

Answer

35 Enforcing the nullification of a works council election is not regulated by the German Works Council Constitution Act. According to German Federal Labor Court precedent the results are void if general electoral principles have been violated in such a considerable manner that there is **not even a semblance of a legally held election.**

III. Rights and Responsibilities of the Works Council

Question 609

What rights does the works council have?

Answer

36 The works council is entitled to information, advisory, co-determination, and participatory rights.

Question 610

What counts as information rights?

Answer

37 Information rights apply especially to HR planning, and the hiring, relocating and dismissal of employees. The law requires that the works council **be informed of every employee dismissal.**

Question 611

What counts as advisory rights?

Answer

38 The works council is entitled rights to advise on **economic matters** related to the company, as well as **operational changes.**

Question 612
What counts as participatory rights?

Answer
The works council is entitled to participatory rights with respect to HR planning and 39
job vacancy announcements. They can also **have a say in social matters** (i.e. rules regarding regular working hours or it systems that may track peoples working habits).

Question 613
What counts for co-determination rights?

Answer
The works council **can challenge the dismissal** of an employee for legally recog- 40
nized reasons. Typical co-determination rights are characterized by being those designated matters that must first agreed upon by the works council, for without the works council's consent, they would not be in force. Other co-determination rights are found, for example, in cases of **operational changes**.

Question 614
May the works council take part in party politics?

Answer
No. The works council is **legally forbidden** from taking part in party politics. In- 41
deed, peace in the work place should not be endangered by an intrusion of differences of opinion about party politics. According to German Federal Labor Court legal precedent, however, **general political commentary is allowed** so long as it does not relate to a specific party. What is not allowed is direct campaigning for a particular party, or activities aimed against specifically named politicians or parties.

Question 615
What responsibilities does the works council have?

Answer
The works council should take care of the employee's concerns, make requests re- 42
garding matters that coincide with **employees' wishes**, and **support and secure the work activity** at the company. Beyond this the works council has to take care that the applicable standards that favor employees are carried out as long as occupational safety and environmental protection are encouraged. Carrying out the **se-**

lection of youth worker and trainee representation are also their responsibility. The works council is further obligated to operate in a **fashion that benefits the company**.

IV. Works Meetings

Question 616

Does the employer have to tolerate works meetings?

Answer

43 Yes, as this is, after all, an **internal company forum** between personnel, works council and employer.

Question 617

Do works meetings have to take place during working hours?

Answer

44 The regular works meetings and those convened per the wishes of the employer take place during working hours. Participation at these meetings and the additional time to the meetings are to be **compensated for as work time**. This then also applies if the regular works meeting takes place outside of working hours. However, there is **no right to compensation for any additional other works meetings**, which often take place outside of normal business hours.

Question 618

May unions take part in the works meetings?

Answer

45 Yes, representatives of the unions for that company can take part in the works meetings in an **advisory capacity**. The works council chairperson has to provide the time, place and agenda in a timely manner and in written form to the union(s) represented at the company.

Printed and bound by CPI Group (UK) Ltd, Croydon, CR0 4YY
13/09/2026
14960856-0001